The Work of the University

The Work of the University

Richard C. Levin

Yale University Press   New Haven and London

Printed in the United States of America by R. R. Donnelley & Sons,
Harrisonburg, Virginia.

Library of Congress Cataloging-in-Publication Data
Levin, Richard C.
    The work of the university / Richard C. Levin.
        p. cm.
Includes bibliographical references.
    ISBN 0-300-10001-9 (alk. paper)
        1. Education, Higher—Aims and objectives—United States.
    2. Yale University.   I. Title.
LA227.4 .L48 2003
378'.001—dc21

                                                    2002152345

A catalogue record for this book is available from the British Library.

The paper in this book meets the guidelines for permanence and durability
of the Committee on Production Guidelines for Book Longevity of the
Council on Library Resources.

            10   9   8   7   6   5   4   3   2   1

Contents

Reflections on the American Economy

Introduction

The essays and speeches in this volume reveal but a small part of what it is to be president of a great university. But they are committed to writing, and therefore they are the part that is most easily revealed. As I approach the tenth anniversary of my appointment as Yale's president, it is time to share these reflections, analyses, and exhortations.

We hear much these days about beleaguered university presidents, overwhelmed by the multiple constituencies they must please, unable to act decisively or speak out convincingly. Nothing about this stereotype conforms to my experience. The job is complex and demanding, but it has its own logic and many satisfactions.

The logic is simple: appoint good people and set clear priorities. At Yale and other great universities, the faculty controls the appointment of professors, our most precious human resource. This is as it should be; only the faculty possesses sufficient expertise to judge the quality of scholars on the frontiers of knowledge. But the Yale president appoints those who lead and manage the institution: six officers, the fourteen deans (of the College, the Graduate School, ten professional schools, and two faculties within larger schools), the librarian, the athletic director, the chaplain, three museum directors, the heads of eight research centers, the masters of twelve residential colleges, and the heads of the thirty-four departments in the Faculty of Arts and Sciences. With the authority to confer major responsibility upon eighty individuals, one cannot reasonably complain that one lacks the power to effect change. To the contrary, one has the capacity to make a profound difference, provided one selects individuals who are strong enough to lead, wise enough to listen, and willing enough to subordinate individual ambition to collective advancement.

For any university president, certain objectives are always paramount: to attract and nurture faculty and students of the highest quality, and to maintain the strength of library collections and other research resources. For any Yale president two additional goals stand alongside these: commitments to excellence in undergraduate education and to the education of leaders in scholarship, the professions, and public life. But when I became president in 1993, two priorities were unique to the moment. Our magnificent facilities, largely constructed between the two world wars, were in an alarming state of disrepair. And our capacity to attract students and faculty of the highest caliber was becoming compromised by the conditions of life in our host city. Thus, our leadership team initiated a renovation program of massive proportions and a series of partnerships with the city of New Haven involving investment in the community on a scale never before undertaken by a university.

In normal times, these might have been priorities enough for a decade or more. But the robust performance of financial markets in the 1990s and the superior management of Yale's endowment by David Swensen and his colleagues made it possible, by the late 1990s, to contemplate ambitious new goals for the university. Several of the speeches in this volume set forth the rationale for making major investments in science and internationalizing the teaching and research programs of the university, as well as the composition of its student population.

The satisfactions of the job follow in part from this logic. Watching people excel is a source of great pleasure, whether it is Alison Richard, our superb provost, orchestrating the recruitment of a distinguished biologist or historian, or Linda Lorimer, once described by Bart Giamatti as Yale's utility infielder, planning and executing the university's spectacular year of tercentennial celebration, or Dick Brodhead, the rhetorically gifted dean of Yale College, speaking anytime, anywhere. I also take pleasure in the physical transformation of the campus and the economic and physical revitalization of New Haven. These satisfactions are amplified by the delighted reactions of alumni who return for reunions at five-year intervals, amazed by what they see. The enthusiasm of our alumni, and their generosity in support of the enterprise, would please anyone but the most cynical.

Above all, it is the daily pleasures of the job that keep me going. The loyalty of those who work at Yale—from those in the libraries and the budget office to the athletic fields and the dining halls—is astonishing. And even more astonishing is the talent. I am inspired whenever I speak with a colleague on the faculty about the direction of her research or the new course he has just designed. What an extraordinary group of people! And if our faculty is a bottomless repository of creative genius, our students are an infinite reservoir of potential. Although I have given up the regular teaching responsibilities I enjoyed for nineteen years before assuming the presidency, I still cherish visiting the residential colleges for lunches and teas, as well as meeting with the leaders of student organizations. I especially enjoyed playing pickup basketball with students on Sunday afternoons, until the sports editor of the *Yale Daily News* broke three of my ribs a few years ago. In the end, however, nothing compares to standing each year at commencement before 2,500 graduates and 20,000 who celebrate their achievement, knowing that, because of what Yale has given them, these gifted young people will make a mark upon the world and use their gifts in the service of humanity.

This book is divided into seven sections. The first stakes out my goals and objectives on becoming Yale's president. The second consists of my annual addresses to incoming freshmen, each encouraging these talented young people to make the most of their college education. The third describes how universities contribute to the wider society through liberal education, the generation of scientific knowledge, investments in their local communities, and expanding our global horizons. The fourth contains my annual salutations to the graduating seniors, urging them to use their education for the good of others, locally, nationally, and globally.

In the fifth section of the book, I discuss the strategies that Yale has employed to improve itself during the past decade. Then I include a series of more personal statements honoring schools, teachers, and traditions that have mattered to me. In the seventh section, I return to my roots as a professor of economics. The first piece in this section, on the competitiveness of American industry, was derived from a course I taught from 1988 to 1990 and written early in 1993, two months before I was appointed president. The second piece in the section was one of fifteen lectures on American democracy, each given by a different member of the Yale faculty in commemoration of the university's Tercentennial in 2001.

Because most of the speeches collected here were delivered for a particular audience on a particular occasion, I have not attempted to strip them of their context for the sake of consistency. One consequence of this decision is that certain favorite quotations and rhetorical flourishes appear more than once.

These essays and speeches have been greatly improved by the insights and advice of my loyal critics. Penelope Laurans and Linda Lorimer read drafts of most of these pieces, and Alison Richard, Jonathan Lear, and, recently, Helaine Klasky read many of them. I am grateful that none of these readers has been afraid to challenge me. The work would have been much diminished without their help.

I am also grateful for the unwavering support of the Yale Corporation in this as in all of my efforts. I thank Rich Franke and Charley Ellis, who for several years have encouraged me to share my writings with a larger public, and I thank especially David Gergen for expressing his vote of confidence with a generous gift to Yale University Press to underwrite the publication of this collection.

My greatest thanks are reserved for my wife, Jane, my most rigorous editor and most devoted supporter. Her enthusiasm for Yale, its people, and the life of the mind shines through to everyone she encounters in her work as teacher and president's wife. How much more fortunate are we, her husband and children, who get the daily benefit of her intelligence, sensitivity, and love.

From the Beginning

Calm Seas, Auspicious Gales

The greatness of this institution humbles me. I am honored to accept the invitation of the Corporation to serve as Yale's president.

I accept this responsibility with confidence that Yale will enter its fourth century renewed and revitalized. My confidence grows from a knowledge of Yale's present and a reading of its past. Time and again in the history of this institution, its leaders have expressed grave concern about the university's financial health and the deterioration of its buildings. Indeed, one earlier candidate for this job, observing Yale's fiscal and physical condition, doubted the wisdom of assuming the presidency of what he described as a "ruined college."[1] That candidate was Timothy Dwight. The year was 1795. During President Dwight's twenty-two-year tenure the campus was rebuilt, and the quality of the faculty improved dramatically. With the founding of the School of Medicine, the college took its first step toward becoming a university.

External pressures on the university are also nothing new. Public support for higher education and popular enthusiasm for its purposes have waxed and waned throughout our nation's history. Forty-one years ago, President Griswold lamented an "indifferent public policy" that made "inadequate provision" for the support of universities. He questioned the ability of the American people to "understand the

Remarks on accepting the presidency, April 15, 1993
1. Brooks Mather Kelley, *Yale: A History* (New Haven: Yale University Press, 1974), p. 117.

3

fundamental aims and principles of a university."[2] Yet Griswold spoke on the very eve of America's most sustained investment of public resources in higher education.

History gives us hope. The present fiscal and physical condition of this university and the pervasive national skepticism about our institutions of higher education should be perceived not as threats but as opportunities. Here on campus, fiscal constraints provide an opportunity to think creatively about the shape and focus of our academic programs, to devise new strategies to achieve excellence. In the wider world, a skeptical public challenges us to articulate for our time why liberal education remains essential to the well-being of this nation. And a skeptical government challenges us to restate what I believe to be very powerful and insufficiently understood arguments for increased public support of basic scientific research.

My confidence in our future rests not only on our history but above all on the people of Yale: our diverse and inquiring students, our generous and devoted alumni, and our extraordinary faculty. To reaffirm the value of liberal education is an especially easy task for a Yale president, because our faculty's commitment to undergraduate education is unique among the nation's outstanding research universities.

I perceive one other profoundly reassuring sign that the years ahead will be good ones for Yale and for higher education. I have in mind the growing enthusiasm among our students for community and public service. The goals of liberal education have always been both private and public: to improve the self and to prepare citizens to take responsibility for the common good. The tradition of public service is a rich and honorable one at Yale, but in recent years it has been overshadowed by the private pursuit of self-improvement and material gain. Now that a new generation has assumed the leadership of this nation, our students are beginning to commit their energies to public purposes that transcend the self.

2. A. Whitney Griswold, remarks on Alumni Day, February 22, 1952, cited in Kelley, *Yale,* p. 434.

As we rise to the challenges before us, as we learn to innovate in a resource-constrained environment, we will conduct the business of the university in the very same way that we advance knowledge in our chosen fields of scholarship and in the very same way that we engage our students in the classroom—by the use of reason. We must engage each other in conversation about institutional needs and priorities—probing and testing each other's assumptions, widening the scope of agreement even as we define the nature of our disagreements. Reasoned discourse must prevail in all aspects of university life, not only among faculty and students but also in our relationships with our managerial, professional, clerical, technical, and service staff. We must all strive for civility, respect, and trust.

Finally, although the university directs its attention to all humanity and nature, its local habitation is New Haven. It is abundantly clear that the futures of Yale and New Haven are intertwined. I intend to work closely with the leaders of our city and state, to lend strength to New Haven where Yale has something to contribute. Yale must be a source of ideas for improving our local schools and health care services, for making New Haven attractive to employers and residents. Yale will be our city's advocate in Hartford and Washington.

In closing let me express my profound thanks to the Fellows of the Yale Corporation for giving me the opportunity to serve this institution which I so dearly love and to which I have devoted my entire career.

Let us go forward with prudence in the management of our resources but with enthusiasm for the challenge of renewing our dedication to scholarship, to teaching, and to the idea of liberal education. As we look to the future, I cannot promise to "deliver all." Nor can I guarantee "calm seas" and "auspicious gales."[3] But I can and do pledge my best effort to enhance this excellent institution, and to nurture, for its own sake and in the service of humanity, the pursuit of light and truth.

---

3. The quoted phrases are from Prospero's closing speech in William Shakespeare, *The Tempest*, V, i.

Beyond the Ivy Walls
Our University in the Wider World

In the second chorus of *Antigone,* Sophocles celebrates humanity: "Numberless are the world's wonders, but none more wonderful than man." The chorus sings of humanity's power over nature: "Earth, holy and inexhaustible, is graven with shining furrows where his plows have gone year after year, the timeless labor of stallions." And the chorus praises our ability to use language and reason to create a social space in which people can debate what is good: "Words also, and thought as rapid as air, he fashions to good use; statecraft is his."[1]

We celebrate today our university—a monument to the achievement Sophocles extols. We preserve humanity's achievement in our collections of books and manuscripts, works of art and architecture, objects and artifacts. We impart an appreciation of that achievement by our teaching and augment it by our research.

My teacher and colleague, James Tobin, Nobel laureate in economics, wrote some years ago that Yale's primary mission is the preservation, advancement, and enrichment of knowledge and culture. He observed correctly that Yale is one of the very few universities in the world with the tangible assets, human resources, and internal culture to make possible serious dedication to this ambitious task. Ours is a very special place. We are proud of our capacity to advance

Inaugural Address, October 2, 1993
1. Sophocles, *Antigone,* translated by Dudley Fitts and Robert Fitzgerald, in *Sophocles: The Oedipus Cycle* (San Diego: Harcourt Brace, 1977), pp. 203–204.

knowledge in the sciences, the humanities, the fine arts, and the learned professions, and we are especially proud that, within the select group of institutions that share this capability, Yale is the most committed to the teaching of undergraduates. At this inaugural, this time of looking forward, we rededicate ourselves to our primary mission and we reaffirm those values that sustain us in its pursuit.

The tragedy of Antigone and Creon teaches that human potential can be fully realized only when the laws of society resonate with the deepest truths about ourselves. This is our aspiration for the social order we create within the university. As scholars and teachers, we live by values intended to permit the full flowering of the human spirit. We cultivate human potential by a profound commitment to free inquiry and free expression. Only through the unfettered application of "clear intelligence" can we advance genuine understanding of nature and ourselves. We ask hard questions and answer them honestly, and we follow reason wherever it leads, however treacherous the terrain. We practice what we teach our students: question every assumption and pursue every argument in the search for truth.

We live also in a wider world beyond the ivy walls, a world in which we bear enormous responsibility. Like Antigone, the university stands for transcendent principles, those that permit the preservation of culture and the advance of knowledge. To avoid the fate of Antigone and Creon, our principles must coexist in harmony with the principles that govern the civil society of which we are a part. It follows that our responsibility is to educate and to lead, to shape the values of the wider world so that they, too, encourage the full realization of human potential.

One of Yale's principal responsibilities to society was enunciated in its founding charter. In 1701 the General Assembly of Connecticut approved *An Act for Liberty to Erect a Collegiate School,* which it described as a place "wherein Youth may be instructed in the Arts and Sciences who through the blessing of Almighty God may be fitted for Publick employment both in Church and Civil State."

For nearly three centuries Yale has fulfilled its founding mission with distinction, supplying leaders to the nation and the world. Fourteen Yale alumni served in the Continental Congress; four signed the Declaration of Independence. Three of the last five presidents of the United States and ten of the one hundred senators now in office have Yale degrees. Until recently, Yale educated more leaders of major U.S. corporations than any other university. Yale produced the greatest American scientists of the nineteenth century (Benjamin Silliman and Josiah Willard Gibbs), two of our greatest inventors (Eli Whitney and Samuel F. B. Morse), the first African-American Ph.D. (Edward Bouchet), the founder of sociology in America (William Graham Sumner), and the father of American football (Walter Camp). Few institutions rival Yale's record in producing artistic, dramatic, and musical talent of distinction—from Cole Porter to Maya Lin. Yale alumni served as the first presidents of Princeton, Columbia, Williams, Cornell, Johns Hopkins, the University of Chicago, and the Universities of Georgia, Mississippi, Missouri, Wisconsin, and California.

We help shape our society through the highly visible and distinguished leaders we educate, and we also improve public life and public discourse by cultivating in all our students those qualities of mind most conducive to the health of our democracy. By encouraging our students to reason carefully and to form independent critical judgments, we prepare them to be thinking citizens for a lifetime. As an institution, we remain committed to this Jeffersonian conception of the role of higher education in our democracy. By encouraging freedom and independence in our students, we help defend freedom and independence for all.

Yale's early-eighteenth-century mandate was to educate leaders and citizens for a small New England colony. By the mid-nineteenth century, our compass had become the whole nation. As we enter the twenty-first century, we must aspire to educate leaders for the whole world. Our curriculum increasingly reflects those forces that have integrated the world's economy and must ultimately, if we are to survive the dual threats of war and environmental degradation, integrate the world's polity. We must focus even more on global issues if our students are to be well prepared for world leadership, if we are to be a world university.

Although the public understands that universities educate leaders and citizens, it is less well understood that universities have an important influence on the material well-being of our nation and the world. I refer in particular to the substantial contribution that university-based scientific research has made to technological progress and economic growth since the end of the Second World War. Scientific advance is the ultimate source of growth in industrial productivity, which in the modern economy is the principal source of improvement in the standard of living. Advances in basic science provide essential knowledge for researchers in industry and open, often unexpectedly, entire new areas for industrial application.

Since the Second World War, research conducted at our universities has led to dramatic increases in food supply and human longevity. University-based scientific research and training have also given this country an enormous advantage in international competition. Despite the widespread belief that America's strength in international markets is eroding, American firms have consistently led the world in those industrial markets in which technology is most closely linked to advance in science. Ironically, the practical consequences of scientific advance are often most profound when the underlying research is least influenced by commercial considerations. The revolution in biotechnology arose from discoveries made in the pursuit of pure knowledge of the molecular basis of life.

Our national capability in basic research was built by the far-sighted policy of public support for university-based science articulated during the Truman administration and pursued consistently, though with varying intensity, ever since. Today, the scientific capability of American universities is the envy of the world. We neglect its support at our peril.

As we seek to educate leaders and citizens for the world, as our discoveries spread enlightenment and material benefits far beyond our walls, we must remember that we have important responsibilities here at home. We contribute much to the cultural life of New Haven, to the health of its citizens, and to the education of its children. But we must do more. Pragmatism alone compels this conclusion. If we are to continue to recruit students and faculty of the highest quality, New Haven must remain an attractive place in which to study, to live, and to work.

But our responsibility to our city transcends pragmatism. The conditions of America's cities threaten the health of the republic. Our democracy depends on widespread literacy, and literacy is declining. Freedom for all requires that those without privilege have both access to opportunity and the knowledge to make use of it. We must help our society become what we aspire to be inside our walls—a place where human potential can be fully realized.

At this time of looking forward, we reaffirm our past: to preserve and advance knowledge, to defend free inquiry and free expression, to educate leaders and thinking citizens, to teach the world around us, to give scope for human achievement, and to nurture human potential. We reaffirm these commitments not merely as ends in themselves, but as means to improve the human condition and elevate the human spirit. Let us resume our "timeless labor." Let us leave "shining furrows" behind.

The Purpose of a College Education

On Liberal Education

We begin together. As you experience the exhilaration and the anxiety of a new home, I experience the exhilaration and the anxiety of my first year as president. We have clean slates before us, enormous opportunities to make a difference, for ourselves and for our community.

It seems fitting, as we begin, to consider just what you are beginning. Your professors will tell you that the liberal education you are about to acquire is priceless. And your parents will confirm that it is, if nothing else, expensive. Let us consider what you and your parents are buying for all that money.

Liberal education differs fundamentally from professional education or vocational training. It is not intended to develop specific skills or to prepare you for any particular calling. Its teachings are more general and less obviously "useful."

Some commentators define liberal education in terms of its curriculum: great works of literature, philosophy, history, and the fine arts, and the central principles and methods of the sciences. Others follow Cardinal Newman, who argued that education is "liberal" when it is an end in itself, independent of practical consequences, directed toward no specific purpose other than the free exercise of the mind. From this perspective, liberal education cultivates the intellect and expands the capacity to reason and to empathize. The first view

Freshman Address, August 28, 1993

identifies liberal education with its content, the second with the qualities of mind it seeks to develop.

These views need not be in conflict. I quote from a report of the Yale College faculty: "By a liberal education . . . has been understood, such a course of discipline in the arts and sciences, as is best calculated, at the same time, both to strengthen and enlarge the faculties of mind, and to familiarize it with the leading principles of the great objects of human investigation and knowledge." These words come from the text of a report submitted to President Jeremiah Day and the Fellows of Yale College in 1827 and published the following year along with President Day's own report on the plan of instruction in Yale College. Note the faculty's emphasis on two distinct objectives: the development of qualities of mind and the mastery of certain specific content. Concerning the content of a liberal education, the document that has come to be known as the Yale Report of 1828 continues: "It has been believed that there are certain common subjects of knowledge, about which all men ought to be informed, who are best educated." The faculty recognized, however, that the corpus of knowledge appropriate to a liberal education was not immutable. The authors observe: "What . . . at one time has been held in little estimation, and has hardly found a place in a course of liberal instruction, has, under other circumstances, risen into repute, and received a proportional share of attention. . . . As knowledge varies, education should vary with it."

As observers and forecasters of the development of the liberal curriculum in America, the authors of the Yale Report were quite accurate. We no longer consider rhetoric and theology, for example, to be indispensable subjects. And, in contrast to our eighteenth-century forebears at Yale, we consider the literatures of living languages to be central elements in a liberal education. Yet the Yale College faculty's endorsement of change in the content of a liberal education is ironic in the context of a report that rejected curricular innovation and retained the mandatory study of Greek and Latin. This irony reveals a subtle truth: though the curriculum is always changing, it is rare to find among the faculty advocates of curricular change.

This example also teaches a more general lesson. It is all too easy to endorse certain values and remain quite blind as to how they should be applied in one's own life. As I shall suggest shortly, a liberal education leads us to question and define our values. But this is not enough. To understand fully what our values mean, we must also test what it means to live by them.

In defining liberal education, the Yale Report gave equal weight to the content of the curriculum and the development of a particular quality of mind. Although the content of a liberal education has changed, the capabilities it seeks to encourage have not. I believe that the essence of liberal education is to develop the freedom to think critically and independently, to cultivate one's mind to its fullest potential, to liberate oneself from prejudice, superstition, and dogma.

The content of a curriculum intended to foster these qualities is not without consequence. Science and mathematics are essential components of any such project, because they present to the student methods of inquiry that are indispensable to the full development of the human mind and its powers to reason independently. In pure mathematics and theoretical physics, for example, one learns how to reason deductively from clearly defined premises. In the experimental sciences one learns the method of induction, how to make proper inferences from evidence. Similarly, the great works of Western philosophy provide examples of how the mind liberates itself from prejudice by the rigorous application of reason to questions of how we know and how we should act

What you read does matter. But I would suggest that we give less attention to the race, ethnicity, or gender of the authors we read, and more to the seriousness with which they confront what it means to be human. Truly profound works from any cultural tradition can serve to develop and exercise one's capacities for reflection and critical judgment. Indeed, if these capacities were more thoroughly exercised in thinking about the curriculum of a liberal education, the debate could be guided by the light of reasoned argument rather than the heat of passion.

Whatever the content of the curriculum and however it may evolve, let me suggest that a liberal education is not intended to teach you what to think, but how to think. For advice on this subject, consider what Thomas Jefferson told his nephew Peter Carr in 1787: "Fix reason firmly in her seat, and call to her tribunal every fact, every opinion. . . . [L]ay aside all prejudice on both sides, and neither believe nor reject anything, because any other persons . . . have rejected or believed it. Your own reason is the only oracle given you by heaven, and you are answerable, not for the rightness, but uprightness of the decision."[1] This endorsement of the powers of reason and independent critical thinking has lost none of its force. The university remains committed to these values of the Enlightenment.

I have argued that the purpose of liberal education is to develop the capacity for independent thought rather than to acquire specific or "useful" knowledge. In this view I find myself allied with Cardinal Newman, who rejected the straightforward utilitarian arguments for support of higher education. But, as Newman concluded with some irony, a liberal education aimed solely at developing the capacity to reason can be defended on utilitarian grounds because it produces citizens who can make a genuine contribution to society.

"Training of the intellect," Newman observes, "which is best for the individual himself, best enables him to discharge his duties to society. . . . If . . . a practical end must be assigned to a University course, I say it is that of training good members of society." Newman continues: "It is the education which gives a man a clear conscious view of his own opinions and judgments, a truth in developing them, an eloquence in expressing them, and a force in urging them. It teaches him to see things as they are, to go right to the point, to dis-

1. Thomas Jefferson to Peter Carr, August 10, 1787, *The Papers of Thomas Jefferson,* edited by Julian P. Boyd (Princeton: Princeton University Press, 1955), volume 12, pp. 15–17.

entangle a skein of thought, to detect what is sophistical, and to discard what is irrelevant. It prepares him to fill any post with credit, and to master any subject with facility."[2]

This theme, that a liberal education best prepares one to serve society, resonates deeply with Yale's historical purpose. In 1701 the General Assembly of Connecticut approved *An Act for Liberty to Erect a Collegiate School,* which it defined as a place "wherein Youth may be instructed in the Arts and Sciences who through the blessing of Almighty God may be fitted for Publick employment both in Church and Civil State." For nearly three centuries Yale has fulfilled its founding mission with distinction, supplying leaders to the nation and the world.

The theme of public service finds a different, more immediate and direct expression in the activities of those who have preceded you to study at Yale in recent years. Last year over 2,200 Yale College students engaged in community service activities in schools, soup kitchens, health care facilities, counseling centers, and churches throughout New Haven and the surrounding region. I encourage you now to join them, and I expect that, when we gather in the spring of 1997 to celebrate the completion of your course of study, I shall encourage you then to keep service to society among your priorities as you pursue your chosen vocations.

To equip students for public or community service is only one contribution that liberal education makes to the well-being of our nation and the wider world. Liberal education is also a powerful force for the preservation of individual freedom and democracy.

Let me develop this argument, because I believe there are two distinct points to be made. First, because liberal education develops the capacity for reason, reflection, and critical judgment, democratic processes work best when citizens are liberally educated. This idea stood behind Jefferson's support for public education, and it was well

2. John Henry Cardinal Newman, *The Idea of a University,* edited by Martin J. Svaglic (Notre Dame: University of Notre Dame Press, 1960), Discourse VII.

understood by Tocqueville, who observed that "in the United States the instruction of the people powerfully contributes to the support of the democratic republic."[3] He described with admiration the ability of Americans to think clearly and precisely about public issues, and he noted especially the high level of civic intelligence among the inhabitants of Connecticut and Massachusetts.

Second, a liberally educated citizenry is the most reliable source of resistance to those forces of prejudice and intolerance that would undermine our nation's commitment to free inquiry and free expression. Those educated to "fix reason firmly in her seat, and call to her tribunal every fact, every opinion" are those most disinclined to fall under the sway of prejudice, to succumb to intolerance. It is no accident that universities have historically been bastions in the defense of free inquiry and free expression, no accident that within Eastern Europe and China they harbored and nurtured resistance to totalitarianism.

The forces of intolerance are not easily overcome. Forty years ago, President Griswold outlined the dangers of McCarthyism. Today, threats to free inquiry and free speech come from within as well as outside the university. Doctrinaire advocates of the "politically correct" substitute a wish to rewrite history for critical self-examination. They, and many of their opponents, manifest little toleration for open-minded debate. The issues at stake need full and free discussion, with toleration and respect for differences of opinion. We must bring to this debate the full power of our intellects and all our capabilities for making critical distinctions and reasoned judgments. These are precisely the qualities that a liberal education seeks to cultivate.

A liberal education will prepare you to be thinking citizens for a lifetime, to subject the claims of all groups and interests to critical scrutiny, to resist those who would substitute the emotional appeal of prejudice for the use of reason. Given the blessing of free and inde-

3. Alexis de Tocqueville, *Democracy in America* (New York: Vintage Books, 1945), volume 1, p. 329.

pendent minds, you will have the burden of defending freedom and independence for all.

You enter an institution rich in the traditions of scholarship, abounding in the joys of learning. But a liberal education is not simply given to you. You must actively pursue it. Take every advantage of the treasures before you. The world is all before you, where to choose your place of rest.

In four years, we beginners will meet again at another ritual celebration to assess what we have accomplished. As we begin together, let us, with open minds and steadfast hearts, dedicate ourselves to the pursuit of light and truth.

The Task of Self-Discovery

Thirty years ago and three thousand miles away, I enrolled as a freshman at one of America's great academic institutions. I must confess that I can barely remember my freshman assembly. I imagine that my university's president offered some stirring words on that stately occasion, but they are irretrievably lost in memory. I suppose that there must have been some kind of reception following the ceremony, but I remember nothing of it except that it was the first time I wore a necktie in four years at Stanford. The second time was at commencement.

Freshman assembly aside, I have vivid memories of my first days in college. Recollections of some first encounters with classmates remain sharply in focus, but especially vivid is the memory of one of my freshman counselors—a lively, enthusiastic senior whose principal academic interests were English, psychology, and the Boston Celtics. Short, stocky, and curly-haired, he spoke to us that first night in a high-pitched voice filled with an energy and a passion that I found electrifying. I don't remember exactly what he said that evening, but I remember exactly what he stood for throughout that freshman year and just how he challenged us.

My freshman counselor had a remarkable appreciation of people of virtually every description. He had an extraordinary ability to grasp and to articulate the essential and differentiating features of

Freshman Address, August 27, 1994

each person he came to know. He was a student of human behavior, vitally interested in learning everything he could about other people. It wouldn't be fair to say that he was nonjudgmental, because he examined everyone with a discerning, clinical eye, but he relished, almost indiscriminately, everyone's individuality and idiosyncrasies. In some ways he seemed to relish most those whose behaviors were most extreme—from the terrified grind who pulled twice-weekly all-nighters to the exuberant young man, now a distinguished medical ethicist, who repeatedly filled our dresser drawers with shaving cream, flooded the hallway with barrages of water balloons, and occasionally hung dead snakes on doorknobs. But, ultimately, my freshman counselor valued most those people who had the self-knowledge and courage to define themselves by their own lights and stake out an independent course.

He challenged us. He challenged us to be as curious about ourselves as he was, to reflect on our histories and our surroundings, and to figure out, each of us for ourselves, who we were and what we hoped to become.

Why am I telling you about my freshman counselor? I suppose it would be reasonable enough for me to reminisce about my freshman year with any incoming freshman class. But I do so today because among you is the daughter of the freshman counselor I have described. And it is my special pleasure this afternoon to try to pass on to you something of what he taught me.

As members of the Class of 1998, you are individually successful and collectively diverse. You come from 28 different countries, 50 different states, and 886 different high schools. Among you are a cross-country bicycle racer, a cattle breeder, a professional tennis player, and a student who has not had any formal schooling since fourth grade. All of you have significant achievements. You are accomplished scholars, artists, musicians, athletes, entrepreneurs, community activists, and leaders. A few of you have already discovered a consuming passion, an interest that will sustain and motivate you throughout life. By serendipity or hard work you may have precociously staked out your identity, found congruence between your dreams and a role that society has available for you.

But for most of you, the task of self-discovery lies ahead, as it did for me thirty years ago. Here at Yale you will encounter new ideas at an astonishing rate. You will meet people with values and attitudes unlike any you have known before. You will be challenged—challenged to think through for yourself just where you stand in relation to these ideas, values, and attitudes. You will be challenged to define yourself, to seek an identity that both incorporates your past and differentiates you from it, to find a role for yourself in the larger society that gives appropriate scope for you to be the person you aspire to be.

When I spoke to last year's freshman class, I stated my belief that the task of a liberal education is to develop the capacity to think critically and independently. Your central project is not only to acquire this capacity but also to use this invaluable tool, which will be sharpened and refined in the course of your education, to define yourself.

Like most young people in search of identity, my freshman counselor had his own personal pantheon of heroes and villains against which he measured himself. It was quite an eclectic lot. Among his heroes was Red Auerbach, the tough-talking, cigar-smoking coaching genius who led his beloved Celtics to nine NBA championships. Among the villains was the commander of the campus Reserve Officer Training Corps, who, in response to my counselor's mild but principled objection to some military procedure, uttered the memorable words: "Son, never let your ideals get in the way of your daily life."

Needless to say, my freshman counselor ignored this advice. For somewhere in his pantheon there were intellectual heroes, thinkers who helped define the ideals that got in the way of and, indeed, guided his daily life. One such hero was a distinguished psychoanalyst who died this past year, a man who can easily be forgiven for spending most of his career at Harvard because his son has been for many years one of Yale's most loved and respected scholars, teachers, and citizens. I refer to Erik Erikson, whose important books *Childhood and Society* and *Identity and the Life Cycle* gave an early and very illuminating treatment of the idea of identity and its role in psychological and social development.

One of Erikson's principal contributions was to emphasize that identity is formed in a context shaped by personal history and social environment. Personal history matters—the nature of your family, the values and beliefs that governed your childhood, and the ease or difficulty with which you passed through the various developmental stages prior to young adulthood. Coming to be your own person requires that you understand your past and define your aspirations both in terms of past values and beliefs as well as against them. For some, a period of rebellion against the values of childhood and family is inevitable, but forming a healthy personal identity requires a movement beyond rebellion to the integration of the past with aspirations for the future. We are each of us what we have been, and yet we need not be prisoners of our past. Each of us has the potential to be something more.

In *Childhood and Society,* Erikson draws on historical and anthropological material to illustrate—in the context of Sioux, Yurok, German, Russian, and mainstream American cultures—how the social environment influences the formation of identity. Here at Yale you can seek your identity in an environment that abounds in opportunities for learning and growth. There are 1,800 courses available to you—a virtual map of human knowledge. We have magnificent art and natural history collections, and one of the great libraries of the world. More than 200 student organizations give you ample scope to explore your extracurricular interests. Yet perhaps more important than these institutional resources are the people you will encounter and the norms that govern this community. Among the faculty and your fellow students you will find many who have histories, values, beliefs, and attitudes that are strikingly different from your own.

But despite our differences, we are collectively committed, by long-standing tradition and by deep conviction, to open discussion, critical inquiry, and independent thought.

In such an environment you have an extraordinary opportunity to learn, to test your values, beliefs, and attitudes against others', to define new possibilities for yourself. Having the time, resources, and freedom to shape your own identity gives you the best possible chance to lead a full, happy, and productive life, the best possible chance to contribute to the well-being of those around you—your family, your community, your nation, your world. The opportunity to become a whole person is not given to everyone. You have it. Seize this opportunity with energy and passion.

And don't rush to closure. Take time to explore ideas and possibilities. You have four wonderful years ahead. You don't have to plan the rest of your life by Thanksgiving.

Another of Erikson's notable contributions was to warn of the danger of losing one's autonomy by over-identifying with a group. Yale College is a place where the tendency to affiliate—with singing groups, drama groups, athletic teams, student publications, political and cultural interest groups, and Yale itself—is particularly strong. This is a great virtue of the institution, and it is reflected not only in the astonishing energy of undergraduate life here but also in the devotion of Yale College alumni, whose sense of affiliation with this place is second to none among graduates of American colleges and universities. But Erikson is right to warn against letting affiliation with a group become a substitute for shaping your own unique identity. There are two practical lessons here. First, though there is much to gain from exploring the common interests you share with others, don't avoid or exclude those individuals with different values, beliefs, and interests. You have the most to learn from those who are least like you; they will challenge you by asking questions you should ask yourself. Second, don't just adopt a role by conforming to the norms and expectations of a group. To discover who you are and to determine what kind of life best suits you, you must reflect seriously on your personal history and on the people and ideas you encounter.

You will not be surprised to learn that as a junior I became a freshman counselor. My copy of Erik Erikson's monograph *Identity and the Life Cycle* was given to me the first week of my junior year—as you might expect, by my freshman counselor, then a graduate student in clinical psychology. It is inscribed as follows: "To Rick, who is now helping others to seek the wisdom in this book."

Twenty-eight years later, I am still trying.

A Serious Place

Yesterday, as you unpacked your belongings, met your room-mates and freshman counselors, and moved from one activity to the next, you probably had little opportunity to pause and reflect on just what lies before you. That's the purpose of this afternoon's convocation. In this grand hall, built at the turn of the last century to commemorate Yale's two hundredth birthday, you participate in an ancient and solemn ceremony of welcome. You heard the power and glory of one of the world's great organs; as the procession began, you felt its bass notes rumble beneath your feet. You saw the university's officers, masters, and deans march to the platform where they now sit arrayed before you, their gowns and hoods symbolizing decades of study and scholarship.

All this announces to you: you have come to a serious place. This is a place where ideas are taken seriously, where study is taken seriously, where athletics, extracurricular activities, and community service are taken seriously, where involvement and moral responsibility are taken seriously. We welcome you to a tradition that has for nearly three hundred years celebrated learning, cherished excellence, and encouraged commitment. This ceremony is for you—the most accomplished, most engaged, and most promising of your generation. We have boundless hope for you, and confidence that you will make

Freshman Address, September 2, 1995

the most of this serious place. It will shape your lives, and you in turn will help to shape its future.

No doubt you are wondering: what does this serious place have in store for us? I thought it might be interesting to answer this question by reflecting on the words of some of those who have gone before you. Such words may be found in the personal essays published on the occasion of a class twenty-fifth reunion. I chose for today's text the reunion book of the Class of 1955, but it could easily have been another.

The Class of 1955—though its members might object to this characterization—was a class like any other. Of course, like the 253 graduating cohorts that preceded it, there were no women in the class. In fact, the first twenty-fifth reunion of a coeducational Yale College class will occur this coming spring, in June 1996, a quarter-century after the graduation of the pioneering women who entered Yale as juniors in the fall of 1969. In any event, the Class of '55 includes hundreds who have made an impact on their local communities, churches, and civic organizations, their places of work, and their professions. Some have made a notable impact on the wider world—the governor of our largest state, a Pulitzer Prize–winning biographer, and several other distinguished scholars, one of whom is sitting behind me—the beloved Master T., the Master of Timothy Dwight College.[1]

What did these graduates, reflecting on their own experience, point to as the essential features of a Yale education? First, they learned to take ideas seriously. Consider this comment by a civil engineer who later became a lawyer: "Yale introduced me to the intellectual world, and to the people who inhabit that world. It also gave me exposure to the really able people of that world. . . . The questions . . . raised in my mind while I was there have stimulated a lifelong search for answers, and in so doing have vastly enriched my life."

1. More fully identified, these class members are Pete Wilson, David McCullough, and Robert Farris Thompson.

You will encounter ideas here. Many will excite your curiosity and open you to entirely new areas of knowledge and new perspectives. You will also learn that there are people for whom the life of the mind is the essence of life. Most of you, like our first witness from the Class of '55, won't choose that course for yourselves, but you will come to appreciate how such people—scholars and scientists, your professors among them—enrich the lives of others.

Many members of the Class of '55 comment how their exposure to new ideas at Yale gave them a lifelong appreciation of literature, philosophy, and the arts. For example, a clergyman commented: "I am increasingly grateful for the quality of my Yale education. Yale taught me how to think and how to analyze, and it led me to appreciate the arts."

Or this from a neurosurgeon: "I enjoy classical concerts [and] traveling to art museums. . . . My Yale education has given me intellectual channels to pursue outside my profession."

Or, as a distinguished literary critic who has spent his life teaching in one of the world's great universities and is familiar with most of the rest, told his classmates: "I remain constantly grateful for my four rewarding—indeed liberating—years in New Haven. . . . I have never encountered an undergraduate education that could match Yale's."

Of course, it is not mere exposure to ideas that Yale will provide for you. As our clergyman testified, you will also learn to think and to analyze. Indeed, sharpening the faculties that will permit you to think critically and independently is just about the greatest gift that Yale can give you. Our teachers will not teach you what to think, but how to think. This feature of a liberal education was much appreciated by the Class of 1955. As a stockbroker observed, "I will always be grateful to Yale . . . for giving me the confidence (and sometimes the ability) to question anyone on anything that doesn't make sense to me. . . . I am rarely intimidated and am getting less surprised at how many times the experts and conventional wisdom are wrong."

There is, to be sure, more to Yale College than the development of one's critical and intellectual capacities. Over these four years each of you will develop your character as well as your mind. For more than a century, Yale has been noted for its "second curriculum," the enormous number and variety of activities in which its students engage. Indeed, one member of the Class of '55, later a well-known journalist, chose Yale for this very reason: "I'm probably one of the few people who chose Yale over Harvard just because I thought the *Yale Daily News* was a better paper!"

You will find here an extraordinary array of activities, and you will find yourselves, like generations of Yalies before you, drawn almost irresistibly to an intense and passionate commitment to one or more of them—to athletics, music, drama, a publication, a political organization, or voluntary service in the New Haven community. In such activities you will learn the value of commitment, the virtues of engagement, and you will develop the capacity to work with others, to lead, to make a difference. Listen to these voices. First, a physician:

> The principal thing Yale gave me had nothing to do with concrete intellectual or cultural knowledge. It had to do with values, with an ethic, a way of being, a habit of mind. I am a "doer"—I can't sit back—and while some of that was in me from the beginning, I think it was nurtured by Yale. . . . My belief that you are on the earth to make a difference, that fighting for right is better than accepting wrong, and that intellectual and cultural pursuits enrich life: no one exactly told us these things, but they were in the air, and I became the person I am partly because of them.

And this from a lawyer and active civic leader: "A Yale graduate should either believe or pretend to believe (1) that each individual has an obligation to give more to his or her community that he or she takes, (2) that the lot of people everywhere can be improved, and (3) that one person can make a difference."

An introduction to new ideas, a sharpening of the intellect, a love of engagement, and an obligation to make a difference—this is not all that your Yale education will provide. It will also provide an opportunity to live among extraordinary people, to learn from one another and to learn about yourselves. A banker from the Class of 1955 put it this way: "The education I received was not just from the classroom but from the sharing of ideas, understanding, and friendship. Learning to live with classmates who had different outlooks and values and to find common ground on which to build respect and friendship was an experience for which I shall always be grateful. That education has enabled me . . . to appreciate that it is relationships with other persons that contain the seeds of true and lasting happiness."

If the "friendships formed at Yale" are themselves an important part of your education, so too is the development of capacity for self-understanding. As one scientist told his classmates: "In our time, Yale did not stimulate any of the questions I have been asking myself for the past ten years. But it did equip me to ask them when I was ready, and it gave me reasonable ideas about how to pursue answers. . . . [T]he liberal education I received at Yale has been—and will continue to be—of central importance in my life."

So we may recapitulate: at Yale you will learn to take ideas seriously, to appreciate the life of the mind, to think critically and independently, to engage actively in something you feel passionate about, to contribute to the betterment of a community, to enjoy the virtues of those around you, and to understand yourself. These are the lessons we learn from the Class of 1955: to think, to understand, and to enjoy—to think (for oneself), to understand (ideas, oneself, and others), and to enjoy (each other's company, the active pursuit of a passion, the engagement with a purpose larger than oneself). But lest you imagine that my selection of these themes is the product of my own idiosyncratic reading of the "texts" provided by graduates of bygone days, let me provide one further piece of evidence, testimony about what was told to the Class of '55 upon its matriculation into Yale College, testimony that bespeaks a reassuring continuity of the values that are most central to this place, testimony that links the speaker, his classmates, and you to one ancient and living community. One final reunion reflection from the Class of '55: "As each year passes, my appreciation of Yale and its value increases. We were taught 'to think, to understand, and to enjoy.' Those were the words, as best as I can remember, from one of our first convocations held in Woolsey Hall in September of 1951. I have recalled those words many times."

Welcome to this serious place. May you thrive here, and may this place enrich the rest of your lives.

Preparing for a
New Millennium

You are the fourth incoming class that Dean Brodhead and I have had the pleasure of greeting. I join him in welcoming you to Yale College and in welcoming to the Yale family the parents, relatives, and friends who have accompanied you.

In previous years, Dean Brodhead and I have conspired successfully to differentiate the subjects addressed in our welcoming remarks. But in your case we have both succumbed to the temptation to comment upon what the Dean has called "the astonishing date of your expected graduation." Think of this exception to our normal practice as "variations on an irresistible theme."

Mention of the year 2000 evokes more than the sense of mystery that attaches to round numbers and more than the hope, dread, and strange behavior associated with millenarian movements throughout history. The year of your graduation also compels us, in a way that no other single year in a thousand possibly can, to think about the future. Thus, I would like to talk about two subjects: how you, as entering students, prepare for your futures, and how we, as a nation and the wider world, prepare for the next millennium.

Freshman Address, August 31, 1996

My first observation, bearing on both these subjects, is that we should not flatter ourselves by assuming that we can know very much at all about the future. I recently reviewed the various papers published at the time of Yale's 200th birthday celebration in 1901, and I was struck that among the dozens of distinguished commentators on education and society, none anticipated the changes that the twentieth century was about to bring.

For example, no one foresaw the extraordinary demographic changes in the population of the university, nor did anyone anticipate the enormous shift in the composition of activities undertaken here. No one foresaw that by the end of the century half of the students in Yale College would be women, nearly half of our students would receive financial aid, more than 5 percent of our undergraduates and more than 25 percent of our graduate students would come from abroad, and the number of students enrolled in our graduate and professional schools would equal the number of students in Yale College. No one foresaw the extraordinary growth of the sciences as a component of this and other universities: nearly one-quarter of all the university's operating funds now come in the form of external grants to support scientific research. Nor did anyone foresee that the university's physical plant would be almost completely transformed, that more than 90 percent of the space currently used by the university would be built in the twentieth century.

Such examples of failure to foresee the future, drawn from the history of our university, can be augmented by innumerable examples drawn from other spheres of life. One of my favorites has particular resonance today. In 1876, Western Union, then the nation's largest communications firm, declined an opportunity to acquire the rights to Alexander Graham Bell's patent on a new device because, among other reasons, it was convinced that the telephone would never supplant the telegraph for long-distance communications! A colossal misjudgment—but can anyone sitting here today tell me, with any degree of assurance, whether in thirty years the bulk of our communications will take place over fiber-optic cable or the electromagnetic spectrum, or whether we will use for this purpose computers or television sets? In the past ten years, the development of electronic mail has restored the art of letter writing, which the ubiquity and ever-declining cost of the telephone had virtually eliminated. Will the advent of two-way video once again make written personal communication disappear?

All this is merely to say that the future is highly unpredictable. But let me say more: this unpredictability carries implications for how you would wisely conduct yourselves these next four years. Most important, you should not imagine that your education is in principal measure to be devoted to mastering a specific and substantial body of information, nor should it be focused on developing specific vocational skills. To prepare for an uncertain future you will need to attend to the fundamentals. You should not focus narrowly on acquiring information and developing skills that may become obsolete. You can use these four years to learn how to learn, how to acquire information, how to develop skills. This means learning to listen and read closely, to think critically, to disentangle arguments, to separate truth from untruth. These are capacities that a broad liberal education in the arts and sciences fosters more readily than a narrowly focused technical preparation, and this is the kind of education to which Yale College is committed.

Just as you, as individuals, must prepare for the future, so must the larger society. It would be comforting to conclude that the political process was adequately serving the needs of your generation, but I have grave doubts about this. I say this not to minimize the importance of the ongoing national debates about values, the proper size and scope of government, and the appropriate rates and structure of income taxation, but merely to call attention to the lack of public focus on, and dangers inherent in, deficient levels of public investment in the future.

Let me highlight two areas of concern: first, investment in improving our system of primary and secondary education, and, second, investment in fundamental scientific research. It is not the slightest exaggeration to say that our society's future level of material well-being depends critically on support for these two activities.

You represent the very best that our system of primary and secondary education can produce, and, indeed, it has been Yale's good fortune to see, year after year, classes entering with ever-stronger preparation and rising scores on standardized tests. But in a society in which access to economic opportunity is open principally to those with adequate literacy and numeracy, too many of our young lack the essential skills for successful careers. Despite the relatively stable performance of the college-bound population on standardized verbal tests, 25 percent of our twelfth-graders and 40 percent of our fourth-graders lack the capacity to read at "basic" levels, where "basic" is defined as partial mastery of the skills required to do proficient work at grade level. And in this age of computers, in which familiarity with basic mathematics is ever more essential in securing and retaining good employment, nine- and thirteen-year-olds in virtually every developed country in Europe and Asia outperform their U.S. counterparts on standardized mathematics examinations.

Against this background it is dispiriting to observe the lack of public enthusiasm for investing in education. Indeed, for the past two years Congress has seriously debated not a new infusion of resources, but actually closing the Department of Education! Now, it could be reasonably argued that, after several rounds of budget cutting, a significant portion of what the Department of Education has left to do falls into the category of intrusive and unnecessary regulation. But is there not a proper role for federal support of elementary and secondary education? We need not abandon the well-established principle of local control over public education to recognize the desirability of a nationwide effort to develop, test, demonstrate, and disseminate innovative and effective ways to teach the basic skills of reading, writing, and mathematics. No state or locality has sufficient incentive to invest adequately in such an effort. There have been some promising initiatives in the private sector, and encouraging these should be part of any solution, but, on the whole, the performance of our schools is too important to be ignored by the federal government.

The second concern I want to raise about inadequate public investment is less obvious but no less critical to the future. Since the Second World War, America's competitive advantages in world markets, and a substantial fraction of the economic growth experienced here and around the world, have depended on a steady succession of technological improvements, newly developed products, and the emergence of entirely new industries, such as televisions, computers, cellular telephones, software, and medical devices and therapies based on biotechnology. These developments are all ultimately traceable to basic scientific research, most of it undertaken in universities and most of it driven by a desire for new knowledge of natural phenomena rather than a quest for results that have immediate practical application.

The time lags from university-based fundamental research to new industrial products are typically far longer than an impatient private sector will tolerate, and the ultimate commercial applications of new knowledge often are entirely unforeseen when the initial, enabling discoveries are made in university laboratories. These very facts have made it difficult for many of our political leaders to see the essential linkage between fundamental, curiosity-driven research undertaken in universities and the benefits that accrue in terms of human health and economic growth decades later. In recent years there has been tremendous pressure to reduce government support for research overall and to allocate an increased share of federal funds to projects and programs aimed directly at producing commercially useful knowledge. The balanced budget plans under discussion in Congress these past two years call for a 20 to 25 percent reduction in the level of support for basic science.

The investment in fundamental scientific research is an easy target for legislators intent on deficit reduction, because the cost of such reduction will not be perceptible in our nation's economic performance over the next five to ten years. But, throwing my caution about forecasting the future to the wind, let me assure you that today's failure to maintain investment in basic science will have a profoundly negative effect on economic performance in the next twenty-five to fifty years.

If these reflections on the coming millennium have strayed from the subject of your entry into Yale College, such is the lure of the round number that each of you will bear after your name in future issues of the *Yale Alumni Directory*. I encourage each of you, women and men of the Class of 2000, to partake in such speculation yourself. Think about the future, boldly and often. Think about the possibilities the future holds for you, not only as an individual but as a responsible and committed citizen. I have highlighted some important matters that we must act upon now to lighten your burdens in the future. But, ultimately, the future is yours to shape. Seize the opportunity to use the vast resources of this place to prepare yourself. Welcome to Yale.

Discovery

I am going to begin with a confession. This summer I got very excited about the Pathfinder mission to Mars. Perhaps it was nostalgia. I was about your age when the Apollo spaceships started circling the moon, and only a little older when astronauts first walked on the lunar surface. The miniature robot Sojourner intensified my yearning for lost youth. It looked to me like something constructed by merging my old Erector set with my children's Legos.

I was captivated by the photographs. I found them even more interesting than the lunar landscapes beamed back by the Apollo crews. We have, after all, seen dusty deserts set against the darkness of the night sky, but we have never seen red and blue deserts set against a red sky. What most enthralled me, however, was a short article I saw in the *International Herald Tribune* while on vacation abroad. It noted that the Pathfinder had recorded a ground-level temperature reading of 70 degrees Fahrenheit, warm enough to go barefoot, while the temperature at an altitude of 5 feet was only 15 degrees Fahrenheit, cold enough for a wool hat. Even without canals and anthropomorphic aliens, Mars turns out to be as strange as we ever imagined and even more beautiful.

Humanity is entering a new Age of Discovery. In the next third of a century we will doubtless learn as much, and probably much more, about our neighboring planets than we learned about Earth in the comparable span of years between Columbus' first voyage and

Freshman Address, August 30, 1997

Magellan's last. I could go on to say more about how interplanetary exploration might expand our knowledge, our material well-being, and our collective imagination. Or I could go on to urge that we avoid the imperial ambitions and the environmental destruction that accompanied the last Age of Discovery. But I will do neither. I would prefer to comment on the phenomenon of discovery itself and how each of you might seize on the abundant opportunities for discovery that Yale will make available to you these next four years.

To understand better the nature of discovery, I turned from perusal of the Martian photographs to the memoirs of some very distinguished scientists. I learned, to no great surprise, that discovery begins with curiosity. I was particularly struck by this recollection of Richard Feynman, one of this century's great physicists:

> My father taught me to notice things, and one day I was playing with . . . a little wagon. . . . It had a ball in it, and when I pulled the wagon I noticed something about the way the ball moved. I went to my father and I said, "Say, Pop, I noticed something. When I pull the wagon, the ball rolls to the back of the wagon. And when I'm pulling it along and I suddenly stop, the ball rolls to the front of the wagon. Why is that?"

It helps, if you are curious, to have access to people who have answers. Feynman was lucky enough to have access to a father who had not only the answer, but wisdom as well. To Feynman's question—"Why is that?"—his father replied: "Nobody knows. The general principle is that things that are moving try to keep on moving, and things that are standing still tend to stand still unless you push on them hard. This tendency is called 'inertia,' but nobody knows why it's true." Feynman adds his own gloss: "Now, that's a deep understanding: he didn't just give me a name. He knew the difference between knowing the name of something and knowing something."[1]

1. Christopher Sykes, editor, *No Ordinary Genius* (New York: W. W. Norton, 1994), p. 24.

Here at Yale you will have access to many people with answers and more than a few with wisdom, a distinguished faculty of 700 men and women with expertise in virtually every area of human knowledge. They will not always have the answers you seek, but they will encourage your curiosity and inspire you to make discoveries on your own. Here is how David McCullough, Yale College Class of 1955 and a Pulitzer Prize–winning biographer, described one of his teachers to the seniors of 1997 during Commencement weekend: "He threw open the windows for us, threw open the shutters, let the light in. He got us to read, got us to think, he got us to see, *to see*, and he's never stopped."

Discovery requires more than curiosity and inspiration, more than access to information; it requires discipline and persistence as well. I used to teach a course on the economics of technological change, and one of my favorite invention stories serves well to illustrate this point. There was a chemist who worked for Du Pont who believed it possible to find useful applications for a polymer the company had patented. After thirteen years he left Du Pont, secured the rights to the still undeveloped polymer, and went into business with his son, using the substance to manufacture ribbon cable. Another eleven years passed, and the chemist still believed that the polymer had important undiscovered uses. If the substance could only be made to stretch, he postulated, it might become impermeable to liquids but allow water vapor to pass through. Such a waterproof but breathable substance would have value in many applications; for example, it might be made into tape for use in vascular surgery, or, less esoterically, it might serve well to seal junctions in pipes. He began to subject a small rod of the polymer to a different experimental treatment each day. The substance was heated and cooled for various lengths of time and then pulled. Day after day, the rod snapped in two. Finally, at the end of one frustrating day, the chemist's weary son, eager to get home, rushed into the lab, grabbed the rod out of the oven, pulled at both ends, and—lo and behold—Gore-Tex![2]

2. Lucien Rhodes, "The Un-manager," *Inc.*, August 1982, p. 34.

As the example illustrates, even years of persistence are not always enough; a certain amount of luck is involved. Francis Crick, the co-discoverer of the double-helical structure of DNA, explains in his memoir that his colleague, James Watson, made a critical inference about the exact nature of the two base pairs by chance manipulation of a physical model of the molecule, even though, in retrospect, it could have been deduced logically. But Crick reminds us that "chance favors the prepared mind." He observes that "Jim was looking for something significant and immediately recognized the significance of the correct pairs when he hit upon them by chance."[3]

I have so far identified curiosity, access to information, persistence, preparation, and luck as elements of discovery. Perhaps I should also add peripheral vision. It is not uncommon to discover something new while looking for something very different. Steven Weinberg, the Nobel laureate in physics, describes how he developed an elaborate mathematical structure to explain the strong nuclear force, realized that he could not reconcile the mathematics with experimental observation, but then recognized that the same mathematics were in fact the key to explaining the weak nuclear force and, ultimately, to developing a unified theory of the weak and electromagnetic forces.[4]

Let me also say a word about intellectual ambition, which I shall count as the final requisite of discovery. Or rather, let me quote at length from Francis Crick, who sums up eloquently:

> The major credit I think Jim and I deserve . . . is for selecting the right problem and sticking to it. It's true that by blundering about we stumbled on gold, but the fact remains that we were looking for gold. Both of us had decided, quite independently of each other, that the central

3. Francis Crick, *What Mad Pursuit: A Personal View of Scientific Discovery* (New York: Basic Books, 1988), p. 66.
4. Steven Weinberg, *Dreams of a Final Theory* (New York: Vintage, 1994), pp. 118–119.

problem in molecular biology was the chemical structure of the gene. . . . We could not see what the answer was, but we considered it so important that we were determined to think about it long and hard, from any relevant point of view.[5]

I should hasten to add that the act of discovery can be deeply satisfying, emotionally as well as intellectually. When I asked Sidney Altman—our Sterling Professor of Biology, Nobel laureate, and a former dean of Yale College—to comment on his own experience, he said:

> When I was a post-doc, I did an experiment that resolved a problem that I had been working on for a year or more. When I saw the result, there was not only the feeling of relief you get when you stop banging your head against a wall, but, more important, I then understood some of the puzzling results that had been published by others in the years before. The feeling of great satisfaction at having solved my problem as well as having illuminated others kept me floating on air for weeks.

I have been drawing my examples from the world of science and technology, but what I have said about discovery applies in virtually every area of human inquiry. Some of you will see flashes of blinding light working in a science or engineering laboratory here at Yale. But others will experience the joy of discovery in the University Art Gallery, in the Manuscripts and Archives Division of the Sterling Library, or in a post-midnight conversation with a suite-mate.

Women and men of the Class of 2001, welcome to Yale College, where the possibilities for discovery are without limit. We set before you a treasury of resources, and you bring with you curiosity, years of preparation, and—we must infer this from your surviving the arduous competition for admission—persistence. All you need now is

5. Crick, *No Ordinary Genius,* pp. 74–75.

intellectual ambition and a little bit of luck, although with preparation and persistence, the luck will take care of itself.

Do not fail to be ambitious. One of last spring's graduates published a book describing, with vivid prose and beautiful drawings, all the known species of trout in North America. Another invented a machine, made entirely of spare laboratory parts, that projects three-dimensional images in space. This patented device may lead to improvements in medical diagnosis and air traffic control. Achievements of this kind are within your grasp if you set your sights high.

Above all, make the most of this amazing place. You have 1,800 courses available to you, a library with 10 million books, three of the world's finest university museums, a devoted and accessible faculty, 1,300 classmates from every state of the union and all around the world, and faculty advisers, freshman counselors, deans, and masters to support and encourage you. These four years will enrich you for a lifetime. Enjoy them. Make them your Age of Discovery.

Westward Ho!

E arlier this month, while on a hiking trip, I found myself utterly absorbed by the book I was reading. As much as I enjoyed each day's trek, I looked forward to evening, when I could return to the unfolding drama. I'm sure you have all had this experience, and I hope you will have it often while you are here, with a library of 10 million books available to you.

Reading is an intensely private pleasure, but, for most of us, there is also pleasure in talking with others about our reading. These activities—reading and talking about what you have read—will constitute much of your Yale experience. So I thought it especially appropriate to welcome you to Yale by telling you about the book that I recently found compelling—Stephen Ambrose's account of the brief, brilliant life of Meriwether Lewis, *Undaunted Courage*.[1]

The book is not simply a life of Lewis. It retells, vividly, the gripping story of the Lewis and Clark expedition to the Pacific Northwest, a journey of discovery that resonates richly with the journey you embark upon this weekend. The book also illustrates the genius of Lewis' extraordinary teacher, sponsor, and surrogate father—Thomas Jefferson.

Let me start by talking about Jefferson, the far-sighted patron

Freshman Address, August 29, 1998
1. Stephen E. Ambrose, *Undaunted Courage: Meriwether Lewis, Thomas Jefferson, and the Opening of the American West* (New York: Touchstone, 1997).

of the expedition. Almost alone among the founding fathers of our nation, Jefferson saw both the value and the inevitability of the fledgling republic's westward expansion. To Jefferson the purpose of westward exploration was not simply to gain commercial advantage over the British in trade with the natives and with the Orient, but ultimately to spread—in his conception, peacefully—the principles embodied in the Declaration of Independence across the continent.[2]

Although he emphasized these commercial and political objectives when he sought congressional support for an expedition to the Pacific in 1803, Jefferson also viewed the westward journey as an opportunity to make substantial advances in scientific knowledge. This ambition is revealed with stunning clarity in Jefferson's written instructions to Lewis. He requests a precise mapping of the Missouri River basin and the territory to its west, detailed demographic and ethnographic description of the natives, as well as notice of soil conditions, climate, vegetation, minerals, and species of animals— especially those previously unknown. In short, Jefferson sought a thorough account of the natural and social history of the west. Even more remarkable than the breadth of Jefferson's ambition is this: Lewis and Clark gave him all that he asked.

Now surely it is not lost upon you that you, too, are about to embark on an ambitious journey. Let me assure you that no one expects you to have Jefferson's clarity of vision about where your journey will ultimately lead. Indeed, part of your exploration here will be to determine the direction of your future course. We offer ample means to aid you in this quest: a curriculum of over 1,800 courses covering virtually every imaginable subject of human inquiry, extra-

2. As early as 1783, Jefferson encouraged General George Rogers Clark, the older brother of Lewis' traveling companion, to lead an expedition to explore the territory west of the Mississippi to the Pacific Ocean. That same year he drafted a report to Congress proposing that new states be added to the Union, not as colonies or subordinate possessions, but with status fully equivalent to those of the original thirteen. With Jefferson's leadership, this principle was ratified in the Northwest Ordinance of 1787.

ordinary library and museum collections, and a distinguished and devoted faculty to guide you.

And even if the end point of your journey is unknown at the beginning, I hope that you will not lack Jefferson's ambition. He sought nothing less than the realization of the young nation's full potential. I urge you to seek the same for yourselves.

Meriwether Lewis was only twenty-eight years old when Jefferson chose him to lead the Western expedition, but he had already managed his family's estate, shown his natural leadership during six years in the military, and explored much of the Ohio Valley. In Jefferson's words, he had "firmness of constitution and character, prudence, habits adapted to the woods, and a familiarity with the Indian manners and character."[3] All he lacked was a rigorous training in the sciences, and this Jefferson, Enlightenment prodigy that he was, set about to provide. Lewis learned from Jefferson's expert acquaintances the Linnaean system of plant classification, the technical vocabulary of plant and animal taxonomy, how to preserve and label specimens, and how to determine latitude and longitude. Jefferson and Lewis also spent countless hours planning the logistics of the expedition and determining the supplies that would be needed to sustain the band of explorers.

You come from forty-eight states of the Union and forty-three countries around the globe, from schools large and small, public and private. Yet you have two things in common with each other and with Meriwether Lewis: the natural ability to make a difference in the world and the proven willingness to undertake the hard work that is required. You have worked hard to get here, and, though you are understandably feeling uncertain about this in the presence of so many other talented classmates, you are well prepared for your journey.

I won't attempt to describe in detail the many hardships and hazards encountered by Lewis and Clark as they traveled to the

3. Thomas Jefferson to Benjamin Smith Barton, February 27, 1803, in *Letters of the Lewis and Clark Expedition with Related Documents: 1783–1854,* edited by Donald Jackson (Urbana: University of Illinois Press, 1962), p. 17.

mouth of the Columbia River and back. Suffice it to say that there were harrowing experiences with white water, treacherous terrain, grizzlies, and gastrointestinal disease. There were some tense moments with the natives as well, though most interaction was peaceful. Through it all, the perseverance of the explorers was remarkable. Lewis was seeking an all-water route to the Pacific, and Jefferson had expected that the portage from the headwaters of the eastward-flowing Missouri to the westward-flowing Columbia would pose little difficulty. Neither anticipated that the Rocky Mountains were four times higher than the Appalachians, that many western rivers moved too swiftly and fell too steeply to be navigable, and that the overland portion of the journey was hundreds, not tens, of miles through mountains passable only from mid-summer to early fall. Still, the explorers persisted in their mission. On the arduous return passage through the Bitterroot Mountains, with his men nearly starving, Lewis took time to record in his journal detailed descriptions of six species of birds and three plants previously unknown to science.

It goes without saying that you, too, must persevere on your journey. Not every turn of the river will be easy, but you will have caring teachers, advisers, counselors, and classmates to help you find your way through the occasionally rough waters. You will not be immune to intellectual crisis and emotional hardship during these next four years, though I trust you will avoid grizzlies and gastrointestinal disease.

As you strive to complete your journey, I hope that you, like Lewis, will be driven forward by your curiosity. On the trip up the Missouri, Lewis explored tributaries flowing into the main river to see where they led and whether they revealed any new species of animal or plant life. On the return east, he split the party into five separate groups to explore, among other things, alternative routes across the Continental Divide. Wherever Lewis went, he took note of what he saw and heard. He identified and described 178 new species of plants and 122 species or subspecies of animals, and he recorded all that he could learn about scores of native tribes.

To get the most from your personal journey, give free rein to curiosity. Open your minds, question everything, gather data thoroughly, and weigh arguments carefully. And if you don't understand something, please don't be embarrassed to ask for help. It is far better to look ignorant for a minute than to remain ignorant forever.

The fruit of exploration—the reward for being ambitious, prepared, persevering, and curious—is ultimately the joy of discovery. And few explorers have captured the excitement of discovery so brilliantly and movingly as Meriwether Lewis. Reading his rhapsodic accounts of the fertile plains, the astonishing variety of life, the White Cliffs, and the Great Falls of the Missouri, we are swept away.

I hope you will approach your Yale journey with the same sense of wonder. It is so easy to take things for granted here. But, I assure you, not every pipe organ in the world sounds like the great Newberry organ that announced our entry this morning. There aren't many courtyard spaces more beautiful than the newly re-landscaped Old Campus, nor classroom buildings more impressive than the newly restored Linsly-Chittenden Hall. There aren't many—I am tempted to say any—university art museums with collections to rival ours. And there are only a handful of universities around the world with a complement of comparably distinguished scholars on their faculties. This place is filled with extraordinary treasures; they are here for you to explore and enjoy.

A distinctive feature of this place is that all who come here participate in its making. What Yale College is over the next four years will depend in substantial part on what you make it. And because you will be so involved in shaping it, Yale College will be forever yours. Your sense of ownership, your sense that Yale is your place, will persist for a lifetime.

In closing, let me read to you a portion of Jefferson's most eloquent description of Meriwether Lewis, written four years after his tragic death:

> Of courage undaunted, possessing a firmness and perseverance of purpose which nothing but impossibilities

could divert from its direction, . . . honest, disinterested, liberal, of sound understanding and a fidelity to truth so scrupulous that whatever he should report would be as certain as if seen by ourselves, with all these qualifications as if selected and implanted by nature in one body for this express purpose, I could have no hesitation in confiding the enterprise to him.[4]

Ambitious, prepared, persevering, and curious women and men of the Class of 2002: welcome to Yale College. Without hesitation, we confide the enterprise to you.

4. Thomas Jefferson to Paul Allen, August 18, 1813, in Jackson, *Letters*, pp. 589–590.

The Spirit of Adventure

This summer I attended a meeting at which Bill Gates, the founder and chief executive of Microsoft, discussed some of the advances in technology that we can expect in the next two to five years. I was struck in particular by a prototype device, less than an inch thick, with a flat screen about the size of a typical printed page. The page of text displayed on this device did not exhibit the familiar, unsatisfactory range of color from light gray to dark gray. Instead, the contrast of clear white background with jet-black text was as sharp as you would find in a printed book of high quality, and as pleasing to the eye. The memory of this device can hold the complete text of dozens of books, and before long many thousands of books will be available for downloading from the Internet. It is easy enough to imagine a device containing two of these flat screens, joined at the edge, with the weight and external appearance of a book.

I don't want to claim that this new "paperless book" will completely replace the book as we know it any time soon. But this example is only one of many I might offer to suggest that we are living through a genuine revolution that has vastly expanded our access to information and is radically changing the way we study, communicate, and conduct our professional and personal business.

This Information Revolution has already propelled the American economy to an unprecedented era of sustained growth, stable

Freshman Address, August 28, 1999

prices, and low unemployment. Together with the developing revolution in genetics—which promises major improvements in human health—the Information Revolution has created for your generation exceptional opportunities for scientific discovery, technological innovation, and entrepreneurship. It is not too bold to predict that the economic and social impact of the revolution we are now experiencing will equal or exceed that of the Industrial Revolution in the eighteenth century, the building of the railroads in the nineteenth century, and the invention and diffusion of the automobile in the century now ending.

I find it notable that the innovation and the risk-taking that drive the Information Revolution are mirrored in our popular culture by a renewed passion for adventure. There is, for example, a revival of interest in the history of polar exploration, reflected in the numerous books and articles about Scott, Amundsen, Peary, Byrd, and Ellsworth that have appeared recently. This year's exhibition at the American Museum of Natural History on the astonishing Antarctic ordeal of Ernest Shackleton, the related publication of Frank Hurley's surviving photographs, and a new edition of Alfred Lansing's gripping account of the voyage have attracted wide attention.

Our passion for adventure is even more evident in the current popularity of mountaineering. Jon Krakauer's *Into Thin Air* is among the longest-running best sellers on the *New York Times* list, and David Breashear's IMAX movie, *Everest,* has played to sold-out theaters around the country. Indeed, with neither extreme temperatures nor avalanches expected, hundreds of Yalies are seen regularly walking across campus wearing guide jackets, parkas, and fleece garments of all description from purveyors whose catalogues portray this clothing in use on remote Himalayan peaks.

I must confess that I am not immune to the lure of adventure. I have read all the books I just mentioned, seen all the movies, and—while avoiding anything that threatens danger—enjoyed trekking with my family in the Alps each of the past several years. On such a trip earlier this month I read one of the classics of alpine literature—Edward Whymper's *Scrambles Amongst the Alps,* first published in 1871. The memoir gives a compelling account of Whymper's explorations and numerous first ascents from 1860, when the young Englishman was twenty years old, to 1865, when, after seven unsuccessful attempts, he was the first to reach the summit of the Matterhorn.

What impressed me most in reading Whymper's vigorous account of his exploits was neither the harrowing dangers he encountered nor the exceptional physical strength that allowed him, when summits and glaciers did not intervene, to cover fifty miles a day walking up valleys and over mountain passes. What impressed me even more was his curiosity, his resourcefulness, and his deliberate application of critical intelligence to overcome whatever obstacles confronted him.

Whymper's curiosity was prodigious. He read the geological literature to understand better the movement and historical effects of glaciers, and he staked out his own position in several contemporary debates among geologists. He gave a detailed account of the technology of tunneling through the Alps and the innovations in railway engineering required to handle steep grades. He also described how ropes were typically used in climbing, offering insights that experienced mountaineers have told me were well ahead of their time.

Whymper's resourcefulness was as notable as his curiosity. He virtually invented the alpine tent, which his memoir describes in detail. And he invented two simple devices to assist a solo climber—a serrated grappling hook for help with short ascents and a simple ring that permitted climbers to recover their rope after using it to secure a descent from above.

Each of Whymper's accounts of his investigations and inventions reflects the power of his critical, analytical thinking, but his discussion of how to plan a route up a mountain is particularly striking. Here he gives a compelling illustration of the importance of acquiring multiple perspectives on an object of inquiry. He demonstrates that certain insights may be gained by perceiving the mountain from afar, others can be obtained by inspection from nearby, and still others are elusive until one actually begins the ascent and observes the terrain at the closest possible range. His discussion is a perfect metaphor for how to attack virtually any scientific, technological, or practical problem.

I relate all this detail because you are now setting out on your own adventure, and curiosity, resourcefulness, and critical thinking are exactly what you will need to make the most of your journey. To stimulate your curiosity, we offer you 1,800 courses, covering the whole range of human knowledge. We have 10 million books, two magnificent art museums, unique natural history collections, and excellent computer facilities. You have the freedom to follow your interests wherever they lead.

As your Yale adventure unfolds, you will be pleased to find masters, deans, freshman counselors, and a gifted faculty devoted to helping you. Still, you must draw on your own resources. You will be challenged—in the classroom, on the athletic fields, in other extracurricular activities, and in relations with your classmates. Some of the challenges will be difficult, and you may not succeed at everything you try. But the great reward is that your Yale experience will be what you make of it.

Perhaps the most impressive demonstration of Whymper's curiosity, resourcefulness, and analytic thinking is his discussion of how, after seven failed attempts to climb the Matterhorn from the southwest, he decided to attack the mountain from the northeast. From this direction, the perspective represented in most photographs, the mountain appears to be utterly inaccessible, yet it yielded to Whymper's first attempt. What led him to take a new approach? First, he noticed that snow accumulated on the steep eastern face of the mountain, despite what appeared to be a slope of 60 to 70 degrees. By hiking to untraveled passes both north and south of the mountain, he confirmed that the slope, despite appearances, was no more than 40 degrees. Second, he observed that the strata of rock in the mountain were not parallel to the ground; instead, they sloped upward from southwest to northeast. This meant that the ledges, and the possible hand and footholds that they offered, sloped inward on the northeast side, making them easier for the climber than on the more frequently attempted route.

In this example there are many lessons that bear on your Yale adventure. You can turn repeated failure into success if you are curious enough, resourceful enough, and analytic enough to look at things in a new way. You have to think outside the box. Don't take received opinion for granted. Look at problems from all perspectives, and use the power of reason to draw inferences. Ask questions, and don't hesitate to accept surprising answers if your observations have been careful and your reasoning has been rigorous.

Seventy-five years before Whymper climbed the Matterhorn, another young Englishman visited the Alps after completing his course of study at Cambridge. Close observer of nature as he was, young William Wordsworth, by his own account written fifteen years later in *The Prelude,* did not attempt to dissect his experience analytically, as Whymper had. Instead, he found in the Alps one of those rare and precious "spots of time"—moments, when considered afterward in calm reflection, that inspire us, or the poet in each of us, to transcendent insight—about nature, ourselves, and our place within nature. Such a moment occurs when Wordsworth and a companion ascend all morning to lunch in a mountain hut, lose their way shortly thereafter, and, when set back upon the right course, discover that they had, without realizing it, crossed the Alps! Only later, on reflection, does Wordsworth understand the significance of his accomplishment.

Women and men of the Class of 2003, during these next four years you will accomplish far more than you imagine now and, I expect, far more than you will appreciate on graduating. I hope that your adventure here gives full sway to your curiosity and resourcefulness, and I trust that the challenges you confront here will strengthen your capacity for critical thinking and prepare you for the revolutionary times that will be yours. Most of all, I hope and I trust that here at Yale you will find "spots of time" to stir your imagination and inspire you for a lifetime.

Yale Time

In October 1701 the General Assembly of the Colony of Connecticut enacted legislation to establish a Collegiate School. Within a month the trustees of the new school had elected a rector, Abraham Pierson, and settled on a location in Saybrook. A few months later the Collegiate School—subsequently renamed and relocated—welcomed its first student, and, since then, new students have enrolled every autumn. This makes you, the women and men of the Class of 2004, the three hundredth class to enter Yale College.

You, and Yale, reach this milestone in a special year marked by three zeros, a millennial year that remains an occasion for reflection on the passage and significance of time. This summer I attended a remarkable conference in Cambridge, England, where humanists and scientists came together to discuss the subject of calendars. Experts on Greek and Roman, Chinese, Islamic, Mayan, and Amazonian cultures described the workings of the various calendrical systems used by those societies, illustrating how the measurement of time at once reinforced and influenced the prevailing institutions of civil and religious governance.[1] In a well-wrought example, a musicologist explained how Gregorian chant was a time machine, a calendar using

Freshman Address, September 2, 2000

1. Liba Taub (Cambridge University), Michael Loewe (Cambridge University), Silke Ackermann (British Museum), Mary Miller (Yale University), Lawrence Sullivan (Harvard University).

the annual cycle of religious observance to connect past and future to the present.[2]

From several distinguished scientists we learned four valuable lessons. First, in thinking about time, scale matters. Evolutionary changes in humans and other complex organisms occur very quickly when measured on the scale of geological time, but they occur far too slowly for us to see them happening during the course of a human lifetime.[3] Second, in astronomy, distance is a measure of time. The farther we look into space, the deeper we probe into the history of the universe.[4] Third, we have made astonishing progress in the precision with which we measure time. In the mid-eighteenth century, John Harrison's prize-winning chronometer had an accuracy of 6 seconds in a month. Today's atomic clocks are pushing toward an accuracy of 1 minute over the entire history of the universe, roughly 1.5 quadrillion minutes.[5] Finally, the human body has an internal clock, geared to the cycle of night and day. From the study of these so-called circadian rhythms one result emerges of undeniable importance to you—you will perform better, even at age eighteen, if you get a good night's sleep.[6]

These scientific findings underscore that calendars, and the scales upon which time is conceived and measured, have a basis in nature, but they are also social institutions, which is to say they are human creations. This seems obvious enough when one asks the question: why is this the year 2000, and not the year 6004 as Bishop Usher would have had it, or 1490 as the Mayans would have had it, or 211, as Robespierre and his fellow French revolutionaries would have had it?

One commentator at the Cambridge conference[7] reminded us

2. Peter Jeffrey (Princeton University).
3. Stephen Jay Gould (Harvard University).
4. Malcolm Longair (Cambridge University).
5. Steven Chu (Stanford University).
6. Craig Heller (Stanford University).
7. Brooke Hopkins (University of Utah).

that William Wordsworth understood the contingency of measuring time; he recognized that the calendar could be created anew by an act of will. In his beautiful lyric poem entitled "Lines written at a small distance from my house, and sent by my little boy to the person to whom they are addressed," Wordsworth beckons his sister Dorothy to hasten outdoors to experience the warmth of "the first mild day of March: each minute sweeter than before." He declares:

No joyless forms shall regulate
Our living Calendar:
We from to-day, my friend, will date
The opening of the year.

Today, in marking your matriculation at Yale, we are, in our own way, engaging in an act as outrageous as Wordsworth's. His year began on the "the first mild day of March"; yours begins today. For the next four years, your lives will follow patterns both cyclical and linear that constitute nothing less than your own distinctive calendar. Welcome, Class of 2004, to Yale Time.

Yale Time shapes in unique ways the nature of the day, the week, and the year, as well as the entire four years of its duration. Let me take each of these in turn.

In Yale Time, the day (at least the weekday) has four parts: classes, extracurricular activities, study, and hanging out, generally in that sequence, although sometimes (I hope not too often) the hanging out part starts early in the evening and displaces the study portion of the day. Each part of this daily cycle is an essential element of the Yale experience. You have an extraordinary array of classes to choose from, over 1,800 courses in all, covering virtually every subject on the map of human knowledge. There are extracurricular activities to suit every one of you—from intercollegiate and intramural athletics to journalism to music and drama to community service, to name just a few possibilities. Each of these is an opportunity to learn to work with others, to develop your talents to the fullest extent, and to test your capacity for leadership.

Classes and activities will keep you busier than you can now imagine, but you will also need time for reading, writing, and reflection. Here you will find Yale's resources not just adequate but staggering. There are 10 million books at your disposal, most of them housed in the Sterling Library—a Gothic cathedral of learning. Beyond this, you have access to rich collections of papers and manuscripts, two of the finest university art museums in the world, a magnificent natural history museum, and abundant computing facilities.

And we don't underestimate the importance of just hanging out. Your classmates come from forty-eight states and forty-four countries around the world, and the lessons you will learn from one another, the lifelong friendships you will form, are no less important than the lessons taught in the classroom.

In Yale Time, the week has its own special rhythm as well, a cycle that repeats itself through the semester and then starts over again. At the *Yale Daily News,* there are five frantic nights each week (Sunday through Thursday), as the editors work long hours to put the next morning's edition to bed. Athletes live, in their seasons, in a cycle of practice, practice, practice, game. For the Yale Symphony Orchestra, the a cappella singing groups, the Yale Dramat, and residential college players, the cycle is a little different: rehearse, rehearse, rehearse, then a round-the-clock frenzy of final preparation, then performance. For the students in Directed Studies, Thursday nights require the rigorous exercise of writing a paper, but the exercise is often deferred until they finish reading the 600-page book they are writing about.

In Yale Time, the year passes by in two repeated cycles, with the long summer marking a transition to the next. Each semester begins with the luxurious practice known as the shopping period, during which you can sample just about as many courses as you can fit into your day before settling on a final schedule. In these early weeks you will find yourself gradually adding extracurricular commitments, generally thriving until midterm examinations come into view. Then you temporarily panic when you wonder, with all that I now have to do, how will I ever make it through the semester? Then midterms come and go. The pressure eases. You start to enjoy the challenge of writing a term paper or two, even as extracurricular deadlines approach—a performance by the elementary school children you have been tutoring, an article due in a campus publication, a decisive intramural game. Then, just as the fun is beginning, it's time to finish those term papers and study for final exams. The semester ends with a sense of wonder (How did I ever make it through all those courses and outside activities?), a sense of accomplishment (I made it through all those courses and activities!), and a sense of regret (What a great semester! I wish I could do it all over again.).

Yale Time is cyclical and repetitive, but it is also linear, moving inevitably forward, in a logical progression, to a conclusion. As you move forward in the progression of years, more will be expected of you, and you will build on what has gone before. As freshmen you will choose your courses from a large menu, cover distribution requirements, and explore a few areas of potential interest. As sophomores you will try out a few more subjects, broadening the scope of your knowledge even as you choose a major. Some of you, especially those committed to science or engineering, will need to make an early decision about a major, but many of you will keep your options open all year. As juniors you will dig in, probing deeply into your chosen major, gaining sophistication, and occasionally pausing to reflect on how much you are learning here. As seniors you will undertake independent research under the close supervision of a faculty adviser—a scientific project, a senior essay, or a major seminar paper.

The same progression occurs in extracurricular pursuits. As a first-semester freshman, you hang around the *Daily News* hoping for an assignment; you get one or two stories in the spring. As a sophomore you are assigned to a regular beat, and as a junior you are elected to the editorial board. Or you sit on the bench as a freshman, get into a few games as a sophomore, become a starter as a junior and a team leader as a senior.

In Yale Time, your four years are a linear progression, containing repeated cycles within them, but they are also a whole, a unity. Taken together, they will be *your* Yale Time—four years that will occupy a special place in your memories as long as you live. You will never forget that first meeting with a lifelong friend, that amazing victory at the Harvard game, that professor who first inspired your interest in cosmology or Chinese history or pre-Columbian art or robotics. You are the most promising young people of your generation, and you will realize, perhaps not now, but later in life, that these four years are a rare privilege—a privilege that you have worked hard to earn, but a privilege nonetheless. Yale provides you with four years of almost unimaginable freedom—freedom to discover who you are through encounter with classmates so very different but equally talented, freedom to discover what most interests and motivates you.

In Yale Time, your four years are very much your own. They will be rich, rewarding, and intensely personal, and the Yale that shapes them, however durable its three centuries makes it, will be, in Proust's words "as fugitive, alas, as the years."[8] You will return to campus after your Yale Time is over, perhaps every five years at reunions, and although you will find Yale familiar, it will not be the same place because it is not the same time. As Proust discovered when he returned to the Bois de Boulogne, "It sufficed that Mme. Swann did not appear, in the same attire and at the same moment, for the whole avenue to be altered."[9] Your Yale, like Proust's Bois de Boulogne, exists as a place only in time, and, once you graduate, it will persist only in memory.

Your Yale Time begins now. It will be yours to remember for a lifetime. Seize it. Enjoy it. Make the most of it.

8. Marcel Proust, *Remembrance of Things Past,* translated by C. K. Scott Moncrieff and Terence Kilmartin (New York: Vintage, 1982), volume 1, p. 462.
9. Ibid.

Beginnings

This summer I took pleasure in reading David McCullough's best-selling biography of our nation's second president, John Adams.[1] Mr. McCullough, a past winner of the Pulitzer Prize and the National Book Award, is no stranger to this place. Exactly fifty years ago he sat where you are sitting today as President Griswold and Dean DeVane welcomed the members of the Yale College Class of 1955. He has been back many times since graduating, most recently to deliver the Class Day speech to the seniors of 1997, to receive an honorary doctorate in 1998, and to attend our tercentennial symposium last spring.

I was captivated by McCullough's portrait of Adams, who struggled, in theory and practice, with issues fundamental to the viability of the new American nation. I was especially intrigued by McCullough's account of Adams' relationship with his fellow patriot and sometime rival, Thomas Jefferson, and I had an experience that I hope you will have many times in the years ahead. I wanted to learn more. So I kept reading. And the more I read, the more I became aware that much of the best material today's historians have to work with comes directly from the letters exchanged between Jefferson and Adams, as well as those Jefferson exchanged with Adams' wife, Abigail.[2] And so I turned to the source and discovered to my great plea-

Freshman Address, September 1, 2001

1. David McCullough, *John Adams* (New York: Simon and Schuster, 2001).

2. Lester J. Cappon, editor, *The Adams-Jefferson Letters: The Complete Correspon-*

sure that these 380 letters comprise a treasure beyond imagining—a learned, eloquent, passionate discussion of history, political theory, theology, and the politics of the day. I thought that I might share with you this morning some reflections on the Adams-Jefferson correspondence and the lessons it holds.

It is, in fact, a propitious time to read and reflect on beginnings, because, as you know, this year marks the three hundredth anniversary of Yale's beginning. We have had the opportunity this year to recall Yale's manifold contributions to science, scholarship, and the creative arts. We have observed with pride that Yale has educated leaders of every persuasion for every walk of life. We have also noted that not every contributor to Yale's history fares well when judged by our current values, and we have documented among Yale's shortcomings its belatedness in opening itself to faculty and students of every race, religion, and gender.

In a certain sense, reflection on our nation's beginnings is especially appropriate as we welcome to Yale College a class more widely representative of the nations of the world than any of its predecessors. For the first time, we have admitted international students without regard to financial need and granted, to all those admitted, aid sufficient to make matriculation possible. To those of you who come to us from other nations, I hope that during your time here you will be challenged not only by the values of this institution—its commitment to curiosity, open-mindedness, and unconstrained critical inquiry—but also by the values of this nation—its energy, optimism, and commitment to democracy.

Adams and Jefferson were comrades in the struggle for independence, and they became especially close friends when they collaborated on a diplomatic mission in Paris.[3] Estranged after the presidential elec-

dence Between Thomas Jefferson and Abigail and John Adams (Chapel Hill: University of North Carolina Press, 1959). Cited hereafter as *Letters*.

3. Adams met Jefferson when both came to Philadelphia as delegates to the Continental Congress in the summer of 1775. They worked as allies in the struggle to persuade their fellow delegates to break from Great Britain. With powerful logic

tion of 1800, they did not resume contact until 1812 after both had retired from public life. Although they never saw each other again, for the next fourteen years the two engaged in vigorous and brilliant correspondence until they died, on the same day, July 4, 1826, the fiftieth anniversary of the Declaration of Independence.

I want to tell you something about the Adams-Jefferson correspondence because it is, in a word, inspiring. I want to tell you specifically about three qualities revealed in the letters: a passion for learning, the capacity for independent thought, and a friendship grounded in the deepest respect and admiration. I hope that you will strive for these qualities of mind and soul, and I profoundly hope that your Yale experience will be as rewarding for you as their relationship was for them.

The letters are, first of all, filled with learning. Adams and Jefferson were voracious readers and prolific writers. Both were fluent in Greek, Latin, and French. Jefferson had the largest library in Virginia, Adams one of the finest in Massachusetts. They suggested readings and ordered books from Europe for each other. They read, and wrote letters about, such diverse subjects as the role of prophecy in native American cultures, the histories of Massachusetts and Virginia, Socrates, Jesus, the French *philosophes,* Goethe's commentary on the Ten Commandments, the lives of the saints, and Plato's *Republic,* which, not surprisingly, both of them loathed. Jefferson, the great democrat, confesses that while reading the *Republic,* "I laid it down often to ask myself how it could have been that the world should have so long consented to give reputation to such nonsense as this?"[4] Adams

---

and rhetoric, Adams dominated the congressional debate, and he assigned to Jefferson, the master of English prose, the task of putting the actions and aspirations of the colonial rebels into words. Early in 1778, Adams went to Paris to seek support from the French, and he remained in Europe on a succession of diplomatic assignments for most of the ensuing decade. Jefferson joined Adams in Paris in 1784 and remained in Europe until 1789. It was during this period, especially between August 1784 and May 1785 when both men were in Paris, that Jefferson dined frequently with John and Abigail Adams and became an intimate friend of both.

4. Jefferson to Adams, July 5, 1814, *Letters,* p. 432.

replies: "I am very glad you have seriously read Plato: and still more rejoiced to find that your reflections upon him so perfectly harmonize with mine."[5]

It's not only the breadth of their learning that impresses, but their passion for it. Adams writes: "So many subjects crowd upon me that I know not with which to begin."[6] On the particular subject of government, where their passion was most intense, Adams insists: "You and I ought not to die, before we have explained ourselves to each other."[7] Jefferson concurs,[8] and later, in his more reserved manner, expresses his own appreciation for their learned exchange: "But why," he writes, "am I dosing you with these Ante-diluvian topics? Because I am glad to have some one to whom they are familiar, and who will not receive them as if dropped from the moon."[9]

Yet despite a common mastery of Classical, Christian, and Enlightenment texts and common experiences as revolutionaries, diplomats, and presidents, each of the two patriots had a powerful mind of his own. Each held religious views so radical that they could express them only to each other, and perhaps to a few other intimate friends. They differed most sharply in their views of government. Jefferson, the eloquent idealist, envisioned true democracy at the most local level, in communities sufficiently small that everyone would recognize a "natural aristocracy" based on talent and virtue, and these natural aristocrats would rise to leadership. Although he expressed confidence that a larger population would also select talented and virtuous leaders, he believed that the powers conferred to successively higher levels of political organization, state and national governments, should be nothing more than the minimum necessary for defense and commerce. Adams, the brilliant pragmatist, wrestled with the complexities of governing a growing nation, one destined—in

5. Adams to Jefferson, July 16, 1814, *Letters,* p. 437.
6. Adams to Jefferson, July 9, 1813, *Letters,* p. 350.
7. Adams to Jefferson, July 15, 1813, *Letters,* p. 358.
8. Jefferson to Adams, October 28, 1813, *Letters,* p. 391.
9. Jefferson to Adams, July 5, 1814, *Letters,* p. 434.

the prescient opinion of both—to span the American continent. Adams feared tyranny, and thought it as likely to emerge from a democratic election as from a seizure of power. He emphasized the importance of multiple sources of power with checks and balances among them. He was never entirely confident that the U.S. Constitution had designed these checks and balances just right, possibly because the task had been left to Madison, Hamilton, and Jay while he and Jefferson were busy in Paris and London.

As passionate and enthusiastic as he was, Adams worried about the future. Five years before his death, the eighty-six-year-old Adams writes to Jefferson. "Must we, before we take our departure from this grand and beautiful world, surrender all our pleasing hopes of the progress of society? Of improvement of the intellectual and moral condition of the world? Of the reformation of mankind?" He reports on ambiguous signals from around the world and concludes, skeptically but not without hope: "I think a free Government is necessarily a complicated Piece of Machinery, the nice and exact Adjustment of whose Springs Wheels and Weights are not yet well comprehended by the Artists of the Age and still less by the People."[10]

Jefferson, the eternal optimist and idealist, responds: "I will not believe our labors are lost. I shall not die without a hope that light and liberty are on steady advance." He notes that the printing press and the wide dissemination of books would alone preclude the possibility of Dark Ages descending, as they did after the collapse of Rome. And he continues, in words that foreshadow those of Churchill: "And even should the cloud of barbarism and despotism again obscure the science and liberties of Europe, this country remains to preserve and restore light and liberty to them. In short, the flames kindled on the 4th of July 1776 have spread over too much of the globe to be extinguished by the feeble engines of despotism."[11]

A passion for learning, the capacity for independent thought,

10. Adams to Jefferson, May 19, 1821, *Letters,* pp. 572–573.
11. Jefferson to Adams, September 12, 1821, *Letters,* p. 575.

and friendship rooted in deep respect and admiration—let me touch on this last of the striking qualities of these letters, qualities which I hope will come to characterize your Yale experience. One finds so many expressions of friendship in these letters that it is hard to select the best example, but Jefferson's last letter to Adams will suffice. In a passage that says so much about their classical learning, their consciousness of their place in history, and their friendship, the eighty-three-year-old Jefferson writes the ninety-year-old Adams, introducing his grandson Thomas Jefferson Randolph: "Like other young people, he wishes to be able, in the winter nights of old age, to recount to those around him what he has heard and learnt of the Heroic age preceding his birth, and which of the Argonauts particularly he was in time to have seen. It was the lot of our early years to witness nothing but the dull monotony of colonial subservience, and of our riper ones to breast the labors and perils of working out of it. Theirs are the Halcyon calms succeeding the storm which our Argosy had so stoutly weathered. Gratify his ambition then by receiving his best bow, and my solicitude for your health by enabling him to bring me a favorable account of it. Mine is but indifferent, but not so my friendship and respect for you."[12]

In praising Adams for his enthusiasm, integrity, and pragmatism, recent scholarship has been somewhat harsh on Jefferson, who is seen, by contrast, as cool, disingenuous, and hopelessly idealistic, not to mention a living contradiction as both slaveholder and author of the Declaration of Independence.[13] Whatever their flaws, I find it impossible to read their letters without finding great virtue in both men. The genius of our American democracy is that it embraces, indeed requires for its success, the perspectives of both: the visionary idealist with faith in the people's will and the skeptical pragmatist, seeking the good but ever mindful of dangers on all sides. We need

12. Jefferson to Adams, March 25, 1826, *Letters,* p. 614.
13. See especially the two most recent books by Joseph J. Ellis, *American Sphinx: The Character of Thomas Jefferson* (New York: Random House, 1996), and *Founding Brothers: The Revolutionary Generation* (New York: Knopf, 2001), pp. 162–248.

both—vision and pragmatism—to propel our democracy. At Yale you will have a chance to discover which of these qualities best suits you, or perhaps you will find yourself, like Lincoln, attracted to the golden mean—holding a clear and steady vision while acting on a keen sense of the possible.

Three hundred years after the first student took up study with the Reverend Pierson, rector of the new Collegiate School in Connecticut, you launch your own Argosy here in New Haven. May your journey inspire you with a passion for learning, shape in you the capacity to think independently, and bring you friendships to last a lifetime. Welcome, visionaries and pragmatists, to Yale College.

Welcome to Yale

You may have chosen to come here because a particular aspect of Yale College appealed to you. You may have learned that our faculty is seriously committed to undergraduate teaching, or that our residential system uniquely captures the advantages of both large university and small college life. Perhaps you aspire to be a journalist, and you heard that the *Yale Daily News* is the nation's best college newspaper. Maybe one of our athletic programs attracted you. Or, possibly, you heard about the abundant opportunities to exercise your musical or dramatic talents. Whatever your reason for choosing Yale, you are about to become part of an enterprise with three hundred years of history. So I want to sketch for you some aspects of that history and give you a sense of the university as a whole.

This is a place with an extraordinary tradition of innovation in education. Yale appointed the first science professor in North America, and it was the first American institution to grant the degree of doctor of medicine, the first to establish a program in public health, the first to establish a university-based school of nursing. We were the first American university to establish a school of forestry, and the first, nearly a century later, to appoint a professor of industrial ecology. Yale was the first American university to establish an art gallery, the first to establish a school of fine art, the first to establish a school of drama. We were the first American university to create a department

Freshman Address, August 31, 2002

devoted exclusively to graduate students, and the first to grant the Ph.D. degree. We were the first to award a bachelor's degree to a native of China, the first to grant a graduate degree to a native of Japan, the first to award a Ph.D. to an African-American.

Yale is a place where the men and women who teach you are international leaders in their fields of scholarship, where seminal contributions to knowledge have been made decade after decade. Yale scientists discovered the laws of thermodynamics and the function of RNA, developed the first interferon treatment for cancer, and identified the cause of Lyme disease. Yale scholars were among the pioneers of the modern study of ancient Near Eastern languages and civilizations, linguistics, and comparative literature, and for the past half-century our literature departments have been at the forefront in developing a series of reigning paradigms of literary criticism. Yale scholars established the field of sociology in America, brought mathematics into the study of economics, and forged the modern theory of democracy. This is an impressive list of intellectual achievements, and the tradition of such achievements continues to motivate the teachers you will encounter over the next four years. Their knowledge and sense of wonder about the world will inspire you. I hope you will take every advantage of the faculty's willingness to engage with you in class, during office hours, and in your residential colleges.

Yale is also a place with treasures beyond imagining. In the breadth and depth of library holdings, art and natural history collections, only one other American university is a close rival. Busy as you will be here with your courses and extracurricular activities, I hope you will soon take an afternoon to explore the stacks of the Sterling Memorial Library. You will be amazed at what you find. As a first-year graduate student studying economic history, I found to my astonishment an abundance of sixteenth- and seventeenth-century pamphlets, published in England, just sitting on the open shelves. And I hope you will visit the University Art Gallery. Take the stairs to the third floor and you will be standing opposite a magnificent Van Gogh amidst an extraordinary array of modern and contemporary paintings. Proceed to your right for a couple of rooms and you will find American paintings and furniture that are among the finest examples anywhere. Across Chapel Street you will discover the largest and most complete collection of British paintings and prints outside London. And don't miss this winter's exhibition of the artifacts of Machu Picchu, the largest ever mounted, at Yale's Peabody Museum of Natural History.

Yale is finally a place with the scale and resources to undertake ambitious multi-year, indeed multi-generational, scholarly projects. No fewer than four monumental projects are currently under way here. Since 1949, Yale scholars have been at work on the publication of the papers of James Boswell, the eighteenth-century British diarist and biographer of Samuel Johnson. Twenty-seven volumes have been published, and six more are in progress. Since 1953, another succession of scholars has produced twenty-five volumes of the works of Yale's great Puritan theologian, Jonathan Edwards, with two final volumes in preparation. Printing the complete record of the important British Parliamentary sessions of the seventeenth century has been an ongoing project here since 1966, and, finally, thirty-six of a projected forty-six volumes of the papers of Benjamin Franklin have been edited and published since 1954.

This past summer, drawing exclusively on Franklin's papers, one of our most distinguished scholars, Sterling Professor Emeritus Edmund Morgan, published a new biography of the learned scientist, publicist, and statesman.[1] Since the year of your graduation, 2006, will mark the three hundredth anniversary of Franklin's birth, I thought I might offer just a few reflections on his life and character and suggest how these might relate to your Yale experience.

I should remind you that among the nation's founders, only Jefferson rivaled Franklin in his range of accomplishments. Franklin was a successful printer and publisher of the leading newspaper in the

1. Edmund S. Morgan, *Benjamin Franklin* (New Haven: Yale University Press, 2002).

colonies, as well as the author and publisher of the biggest commercial success of his time, *Poor Richard's Almanac*. He invented the Franklin stove, made major contributions to the scientific understanding of electricity, discovered that lightning was an electrical phenomenon and designed means of protecting buildings against it. He founded Pennsylvania's first lending library, the American Philosophical Society, the University of Pennsylvania, the Pennsylvania Hospital, a volunteer fire association, and a fire insurance company. He drafted a plan for unifying the colonies in 1754, and then, twenty-one years later, drafted the Articles of Confederation. He represented first Pennsylvania, then several colonies, then the united colonies as ambassador to Britain, negotiated the Treaty of Paris ending the American Revolution, and returned to attend the Constitutional Convention, where he gave the closing speech urging the unanimous support of the delegates. His last public document, in 1790, was a petition to Congress urging the abolition of slavery.

No one expects you to match this astonishing record, but several of Franklin's personal qualities are worthy of your emulation. First among these traits I would cite his relentless curiosity. Professor Morgan recounts that Franklin was constantly seeking explanations for the natural phenomena we observe in our daily lives. He wondered where the air that went up chimneys came from, and he used his findings to improve the design of wood-burning stoves and chimneys. He wondered why oil droplets held their shape on solid surfaces but spread to a thin film on water. He speculated on the movement of storm systems and interrogated travelers to document their course. And, of course, he was the first to explore and classify which materials conduct electricity and which don't. When he grew restless on his seven crossings of the Atlantic, he charted the location of the Gulf Stream, and he designed new hulls and riggings for sailing vessels, as well as propellers and pumps to activate them. He worked with Noah Webster on devising more phonetic spellings for English words, and he advised Robert Fulton on adapting the steam engine for use in ships. He rarely sat in meetings without doodling, sometimes designing elaborate math puzzles such as the 16-by-16 magic square reproduced in Professor Morgan's biography.[2]

Two other characteristics that deserve your attention are Franklin's tenacity in maintaining an independent point of view, and, at the same time, his willingness to modify his opinions in the face of evidence. Throughout the many years he served in London representing the interest of Pennsylvania and other colonies, Franklin held to the view that the colonies should remain part of the British Empire but that their own elected assemblies should have exclusive power to make their laws. Even as late as January 1775 he worked with allies in Britain to put a bill before the House of Lords that would have recognized the Continental Congress, repealed the laws it opposed, and barred future taxation without its consent. The bill was immediately rejected, and soon afterward Franklin headed home. When he docked in Philadelphia in May 1775, he was appalled to learn of the violence of the British reaction to the uprisings at Lexington and Concord. He quickly came to the view that saving the empire was no longer feasible or desirable, and within weeks he was working quietly and forcefully to move his colleagues in the Continental Congress toward a declaration of independence.

Finally, I would note one other admirable characteristic of Franklin—his devotion to public service. Even his science gratified him most when it produced tangible public benefits. Discussing in his *Autobiography* the wide use of the Franklin stove, he reflected: "We should be glad to serve others by any Invention of ours."[3] He initially despaired that his electrical experiments had discovered nothing of use to mankind, but soon afterward he invented the lightning rod.

And so I leave you with these thoughts. When you graduate, in 2006, the tercentennial of Benjamin Franklin's birth, I hope you will look back on your Yale experience with the recognition that here you

2. Ibid., p. 37.
3. *The Autobiography of Benjamin Franklin* (New Haven: Yale University Press, 1964), p. 192, cited in Morgan, *Franklin,* p. 28.

were able to accomplish these four things: to give free rein to your curiosity, to develop independent ideas, to remain open-minded in the face of evidence, and to prepare yourselves not only for lives of personal satisfaction and professional achievement but also for service to others. This is no small agenda, but all of Yale's resources are yours for the next four years. Judging from the experience of those who have preceded you, I think I can say this: you will be amazed and delighted by this place. Welcome to Yale.

The University's Role in Society

Universities and
Our Common Wealth

I t is always a pleasure to come home to San Francisco, and it is a special pleasure to speak in this distinguished forum, the Commonwealth Club, where so many leaders have addressed topics of great concern to the nation and the world.

I speak today of one element of our "common wealth"—the cultural heritage we share. I speak, in particular, of the contribution of our nation's colleges and universities to the preservation and augmentation of that common wealth.

I speak at a time when the value of that contribution is questioned by many of our citizens. Some worry—anxiously and very publicly—that our finest schools undermine, rather than preserve, our cultural heritage. And even those who understand and admire the accomplishments of our universities are concerned that higher education may be a luxury that we cannot afford.

What leads me to say that the public questions the mission and performance of our universities? As an economist, it is my habit to look first at the numbers. Presumably, in a democracy, we can learn something about the public's will from the pattern of public expenditures.

Based on a speech delivered to the Commonwealth Club of California, in San Francisco, May 10, 1995. A revised and shortened version of this talk was delivered as my 1995 Baccalaureate Address.

Consider the government's support for students. In the mid-1970s the average federal grant awarded to qualified undergraduates around the country reached its highest point in inflation-adjusted dollars; it has declined more or less steadily since then. In 1978 the federal government contributed twenty-five cents of every dollar of grant aid awarded by Yale College. Today the government contributes only seven cents of every dollar. At the small number of schools that share Yale's commitment to fund the full financial need of all admitted students, the shortfall in grant aid is covered by the institution's own resources. For most college students around the country, however, the reduced availability of federal grants has led to increased dependence on student loans. To make matters worse, Congress now threatens to eliminate the long-standing policy of forgiving interest on federal loans during the period a student is still enrolled in school. Elimination of this in-school interest subsidy would raise the ultimate debt burden facing many of our college graduates by 25 to 60 percent.

Consider also public support for university-based scientific research. Although aggregate funding has grown at about 5 percent a year since 1978, a closer look reveals two indications of diminished confidence in our universities. First, there has been some movement away from support for the type of basic or fundamental scientific investigation in which universities have unique competence. This has been accompanied by increased emphasis on research that offers greater possibilities for immediate practical or commercial application.

Second, both Congress and the Executive Branch have begun to challenge the principle that has governed national science policy since the late 1940s—that universities, subject to careful auditing and a competitive system of peer review, should recover the full cost of federally sponsored scientific research. Increasingly, academic institutions have been forced to rely on their own resources to support scientific research, and an increasing share of research dollars has been allocated through pork-barrel politics instead of competition on the merits.

Where else do we find evidence of public skepticism about the mission and performance of our universities? In our newspapers and news magazines, on talk shows, in letters from alumni, in the halls of Congress, even in some of our most prestigious journals of opinion, we see a number of complaints repeated frequently: the cost of a college education is too high; professors don't spend enough time teaching; universities should be doing more for the communities that surround them. There are important things to say about each of these issues, but let me focus instead on two particular complaints about the nature and quality of undergraduate education in America.

One widely held concern is that after four years of college, graduates aren't prepared to do anything useful. Although this claim would seem to be refuted by the abundant evidence that the rate of return to a college education increased dramatically during the 1980s, consider this statement from John McArthur, the retiring dean of Harvard Business School: "In Northern Europe or Japan, they have technical high schools that focus on real careers in real industries, giving world-class technical education followed by apprenticeship programs. Students end up in their early 20s able to compete with all comers in the world. Here people go on to something called college, and chances are good after they finish that they are no closer to a [good career] than they were before."[1]

A second concern, perhaps less widely held but even more fervently expressed, is that students are encouraged, even bullied, by their teachers to reject the cultural heritage of Western civilization, to shun the great books of the West in the name of multiculturalism, and to accept "politically correct" orthodoxies. This concern is voiced frequently on the editorial pages of the *Wall Street Journal,* and in letters to university presidents. The dangers of politicizing the curriculum and relaxing standards of critical judgment have also been described by many thoughtful commentators within the academy— among them David Bromwich, professor of English at Yale, whose

1. Interview in the *Wall Street Journal,* March 13, 1995.

brilliant book of essays, *Politics by Other Means*, I would recommend to anyone interested in understanding the culture wars, and Harold Bloom, Sterling Professor of the Humanities at Yale, whose remarkable book entitled *The Western Canon* I would recommend to anyone who can read.

Let me try to place contemporary doubts about our universities in proper historical context. Indeed, the two themes I have identified—skepticism about the practical utility of a college education and fear that universities might undermine prevailing values—are recurrent ones in American history. Tocqueville was among the first to observe closely the distinctively American skepticism about the value of knowledge for its own sake. He noted that Americans pursued scientific knowledge eagerly, but not to edify the intellect. Rather, they sought knowledge as a means to material and physical comfort. As he put it, rather bluntly: "In aristocratic ages science is more particularly called upon to furnish gratification to the mind; in democracies, to the body."[2]

Ambivalence about intellectual pursuits divorced from practical, material ends and concern about the morally corrosive effects of such pursuits have been persistent features of American culture. Motivated by the hostility shown to intellectuals during the McCarthy investigations of the 1950s, Richard Hofstadter published his Pulitzer Prize–winning history, *Anti-Intellectualism in American Life*, in which he traced the roots of our national skepticism about learning to the evangelicalism of the Great Awakening, through subsequent religious revivals, Jacksonian democracy, and recurrent outbursts of populism. He concluded that "anti-intellectualism is, in fact, older than our national identity. . . . Regard for intellectuals in the United States has not moved steadily downward . . . , but is subject to cyclical fluctuations."[3]

2. Alexis de Tocqueville, *Democracy in America* (New York: Vintage, 1945), volume 2, p. 46.
3. Richard Hofstadter, *Anti-Intellectualism in American Life* (New York: Vintage, 1962), p. 6.

The uniquely mixed American system of higher education reflects the national ambivalence about the life of the mind. The land grant colleges, which have grown to become our great public universities, were founded with the presumption that they would contribute directly to the useful arts, especially agriculture, through practical, results-oriented experimentation and dissemination, and their instructional methods were directed toward the education of pragmatic citizen-farmers. The older private universities and liberal arts colleges, though not unaffected by the American proclivity for pragmatism, were much closer in purpose and method to their European ancestors.[4] Indeed, there is a direct line of influence running from the medieval University of Paris to Oxford to Cambridge to Harvard to Yale, and from Yale to Princeton, Columbia, Williams, Cornell, Johns Hopkins, and the University of Chicago, among others.

Against this historical background, let me respond to these characteristically American fears about our universities by asking first: what is the case for education divorced from immediate practical ends? Or, in other words, how can a liberal education be justified today? Then I shall proceed to discuss the second issue: what should be the content of the curriculum?

Although Cardinal Newman had distinctly different ideas about truth and moral development than many who work in universities today, his definition of a liberal education remains highly relevant. As he stated in his classic work, *The Idea of a University,* education is "liberal" when it is an end in itself, independent of practical consequences, directed to no specific purpose other than the free exercise of the mind.[5] Liberal education cultivates the intellect and expands the capacity to reason and to empathize. Its object is not to convey

4. In her recent inaugural address, my colleague Judith Rodin emphasized that the University of Pennsylvania was something of an exception among early American private institutions. Its founding purposes reflected Benjamin Franklin's interest in the useful arts more than the European interest in the life of the mind.
5. John Henry Cardinal Newman, *The Idea of a University,* edited by Martin J. Svaglic (Notre Dame: University of Notre Dame Press, 1960), Discourse V.

any particular content, but to develop certain qualities of mind—the ability to think critically and independently, to liberate oneself from prejudice, superstition, and dogma.

Although the purpose of a liberal education is to develop habits of mind and not to acquire specific or "useful" knowledge, even Cardinal Newman recognized that liberal education could be defended on utilitarian grounds because it produces citizens who can make a genuine contribution to society.

"Training of the intellect," Newman observes, "which is best for the individual himself, best enables him to discharge his duties to society. . . . If . . . a practical end must be assigned to a University course, I say it is that of training good members of society." Newman continues: "It is the education which gives a man a clear conscious view of his own opinions and judgments, a truth in developing them, an eloquence in expressing them, and a force in urging them. It teaches him to see things as they are, to go right to the point, to disentangle a skein of thought, to detect what is sophistical, and to discard what is irrelevant. It prepares him to fill any post with credit, and to master any subject with facility."[6]

Is this case as compelling today as it was one hundred and fifty years ago, when Newman advanced it? I think it is. Of course, one might argue that in the Age of Information a properly educated person needs to master a specific and substantial body of information. But I would disagree. Indeed, the hallmark of the Age of Information is the astonishing ease with which one can acquire the information one needs when one needs it. The capacity to make fruitful use of vast quantities of information is what we really want our students to acquire. And that is precisely the object of a liberal education: to develop the capacity to reason independently, to sift through information and extract what is useful and, to use Newman's words, "to discard what is irrelevant." Presumably one does not wish to produce businessmen and women who know nothing more than the technical

6. Newman, *Idea of a University*, Discourse VII.

tools of accounting and finance, or politicians who know nothing more than the techniques of effective communication. One hopes that the leaders of the next century will have the ability to think independently and creatively, and that they will have formed that ability in the course of reflecting on questions broader than those involved in mastering the technologies of their respective callings.

This brings us to the next question: what should be the content of a curriculum designed to provide a liberal education? There is a widely publicized view that American higher education has rejected the wisdom found in the great works of Western civilization as irrelevant, culturally biased, and politically incorrect. This view not only fails to grasp what is actually going on in our universities; it also fails to grasp what is going on in the great works of Western civilization.

In fact, the great works of Western philosophy and political theory provide the intellectual foundation, and the subtlest critiques, of the institutions that dominate the economy and society in which we live: representative government, the rule of law, individual rights, free markets. This alone suffices to make the Western tradition an essential subject of study. But it is also true that we, and I mean "we" to be inclusive of all literate human beings, understand and realize ourselves more completely as persons if we read and confront the great works of Western literature. None of us is Oedipus or Hamlet or Emma Woodhouse or Anna Karenina, but their existence enriches ours, posing for us in human terms the most profound questions of morality and aesthetics, providing representations in terms of which we define ourselves.

Now it is true that even at Yale some scholars and teachers choose to emphasize the darker side of Western history—the institution of slavery, the subordination of women, the conquest and destruction of native cultures, and environmental degradation. These are, after all, features of our history, and they need to be confronted and understood. The subjects of race, gender, and colonialism elicit strong, sometimes irrational reactions from those who sympathize with the historically disadvantaged, and they surely are worthy of study. But this is not to say that the lenses of race, gender, and colonialism are the only ones through which Western experience is or should be seen nowadays, and they are certainly not the exclusive, nor the prevailing, perspective from which the West is regarded in the bulk of Yale's courses. Instead, old-fashioned as it may seem, most of our undergraduate courses on Shakespeare or Wordsworth, Plato or Kant still wrestle with the question: what is the author trying to tell us about human experience?

We should of course be deeply concerned about excessive politicizing of the curriculum, about choosing literary, historical, and philosophical texts for the "correctness" of their point of view rather than their inherent quality. Yet many of those who fear that our students are being indoctrinated by the so-called politically correct have a terribly naive view of what it means to study Western civilization. They believe that studying Western culture is akin to taking an oral vaccine: by ingesting the great works of the Western tradition and "appreciating" them, one absorbs the values located therein and resists infection by foreign ideas.

We should remember that the great works of the West, taken as a whole, do not present a unified system of values. They converse with one another. Aristotle responds to Plato as Virgil responds to Homer as Milton responds to Virgil. Indeed, as my Yale colleague Harold Bloom argues, all strong poets define themselves against a predecessor, a "poetic father." But a common feature of the canonical works is what Bloom calls their strangeness, their profound originality. Each focuses on the human condition through a different lens.

Nor are these works, taken individually, didactic. They don't contain a doctrine, a codification of values, a set of precepts about how one should live. We don't look to them for practical advice. We don't come away from a reading of *Oedipus Rex* determined to ask for identification the next time we find it necessary to slay a stranger we encounter on the road. As Socrates observed, virtue is not a craft. One cannot learn how to live the good life from an instruction manual; it requires active engagement, thinking for oneself about one's situation.

Why then are the Great Books great? They are great precisely because they challenge us to think for ourselves. They wrestle with the deepest and most difficult questions concerning human experience and moral behavior, and they are so rich in their characterization of that experience and behavior that they are open to profound differences in interpretation. They challenge us, each individual and each generation, to reinterpret them so that they become part of our own view of humanity and the world. And this, of course, is exactly why the great works of the West deserve a central role in the curriculum of a liberal education. Unlike works that are less enduring or more limited in scope, and because they are so challenging and problematic, the great works of the Western tradition are ideal materials for developing the reader's capacity to think rigorously and independently. And the development of this capacity is, as a long line of educators descended from Cardinal Newman has claimed, the principal object of liberal education.

At the core of America's ambivalence about the mission of its universities is an apparent contradiction in expectations. Americans expect universities to preserve the cultural heritage, to pass it on to the next generation, and to educate the young to assume responsible positions of leadership. Thus, the public expects universities to perform the work of socialization. But it also expects universities to be oases of free inquiry and free expression, safe harbors wherein the young can test their ideas, experiment, and explore. How can Americans be confident that, given the luxury of freedom to question everything, the young will resist the temptation to overthrow the established order and emerge as responsible citizens?

Thomas Jefferson's answer was simple: in a regime of unfettered inquiry guided by reason, truth emerges. Thus, we should accept the conclusions of free and autonomous individuals of good will. Of course, we run the risk that received values and beliefs will be rejected. But educators can minimize the risk of unwise decisions by strengthening each individual's capacity to reason and by protecting free inquiry and open debate.

Perhaps Jefferson's answer seems a little too simple today. Perhaps we are a little more skeptical than our Enlightenment forebears. But is there a serious alternative? Ultimately, the reason we believe in the mission of our universities is no different from the reason we believe in democracy. The fear that students will abuse their freedom by rejecting what is best in the culture they inherit is really no different from the fear that voters will abuse their freedom by electing the incompetent, the demagogue, or the tyrant. Can we really trust the people's judgment? Here, too, the answer is that having faith in the judgment of free, autonomous individuals is better than the alternative, which is certain tyranny.

I close by asking: what should the American university seek to accomplish in the twenty-first century? Are not the words of Jefferson still apt? Should we not seek "to develop the reasoning faculties of our youth, [to] enlarge their minds, . . . And, generally, to form them to habits of reflection and correct action, rendering them examples of virtue to others, and of happiness within themselves"?[7]

---

7. Thomas Jefferson, *Report of the Commissioners for the University of Virginia, meeting on Rockfish Gap, on the Blue Ridge, to the Legislature of the State,* August 1–4, 1818, in *The Complete Jefferson,* p. 1098.

The American University as an Engine of Economic Growth

In the mid-1980s, when U.S. trade deficits first reached the level of $100 billion annually and many were questioning the long-term competitive viability of the nation's industries, I offered a seminar for Yale College seniors entitled "The International Competitiveness of U.S. Manufacturing." I asked each student to choose a particular industry and make a report to the class on all the available indicators of the competitive status of U.S. firms in world markets: sales, employment, productivity growth, market share, exports, imports, and patents obtained, among others. The students were required to collect data for the United States, Germany, and Japan over a time span extending from 1960 to the mid-1980s.

The results were very revealing. The data that the students collected indicated that the alleged decline in U.S. global competitiveness was largely concentrated in a handful of industrial sectors. In essence, the United States had suffered an enormous absolute and comparative decline in the performance of two industries that were the nation's largest employers in the 1960s, automobiles and steel. But in most other sectors of manufacturing we were holding our own, and in those sectors with technologies most closely linked to recent advances in scientific knowledge—pharmaceuticals, specialty

Based on a speech delivered to the Asia Society, Hong Kong, October 7, 1998 chemicals, and segments of the electronics industry—America led the world.

Competitive advantage based on the innovative application of new scientific knowledge—this has been the key to American economic success for at least the past quarter-century. And the pattern has not changed. America remains the world's leader in the industries where science-based technologies are changing rapidly—software, communications equipment, and biotechnology. As technologies mature, labor cost, quality control, and other factors become more important in determining competitive success, and the United States tends to lose its comparative advantage. The dynamic sectors of the American economy—where new jobs are created and productivity growth is most rapid—remain those that create innovative products based on the application of recent scientific knowledge.

As the nation's principal locus of basic scientific research, our universities play a key role in this pattern of economic competitiveness and growth. Basic research, by definition, is motivated purely by curiosity and the quest for knowledge, without a clear, practical, commercial objective. Yet basic research is the source from which all commercially oriented applied research and development ultimately flows. I say ultimately because it often takes decades before the commercial implications of an important scientific discovery are fully realized. The commercial potential of a particular discovery is often unanticipated, and it often extends to many economically unrelated industries and applications. In other words, the development of innovative, commercial products that occurs today depends on advances in basic research achieved ten, twenty, or fifty years ago—most often without any idea of the eventual consequences.

U.S. academic institutions now spend over $30 billion annually on research. Nearly 70 percent of these expenditures are directed toward basic research. Over the past three decades, academic institutions have accounted for approximately half of the total basic research undertaken in the United States.

The universities' role as America's primary basic research machine did not come about by accident. A half-century ago, in the aftermath of World War II and as the Cold War was beginning, the U.S. government clearly and self-consciously established an unprecedented and heavily subsidized system of support of scientific research, in the process transforming the nature and scope of the American university. First articulated by Vannevar Bush, President Harry Truman's science adviser, in a deservedly famous 1946 report entitled *Science: The Endless Frontier,* this system has three central features, all of which remain largely intact.

First, the federal government shoulders the principal responsibility for the financial support of basic scientific research. Second, universities—rather than government laboratories, nonteaching research institutes, or private industry—are the primary institutions in which this government-funded research is undertaken. And third, although the federal budgetary process determines the total amount available to support research in various fields of science, most funds are allocated not according to commercial or political considerations but through an intensely competitive process of review conducted by independent scientific experts who judge the quality of proposals according to their scientific merit alone. Within constraints set by the overall budget, there is a virtual free market in ideas.

This system of organizing science has been, on its own terms and from an international comparative perspective, an extraordinary success. There is little doubt that the United States is the world's leader in basic research. Over the past three decades the U.S. has been the source of about one-third of all scientific publications worldwide. Since 1975 more than 60 percent of the world's Nobel prizes have been awarded to Americans or to foreign nationals working in American universities. It is also clear that publicly funded basic science has been critical to scientific and technological innovation. A recent study prepared for the National Science Foundation found that 73 percent of the main science papers cited in industrial patents granted in the

United States were based on research financed by government or nonprofit agencies and carried out in large part in university laboratories.

It is unlikely that this success could be duplicated by industry. The private sector has little incentive to invest in basic research because the returns from the creation of new generic knowledge are difficult to appropriate for private benefit. In contrast, it is much easier to reap the returns from investment in applied research directed toward a specific commercial end, especially if the legal framework governing intellectual property provides effective protection against the imitation of one's products by rivals.

Moreover, the time lags between the initiation of basic (or even long-term applied) research and commercial application are lengthy, far longer than an impatient private sector could tolerate. Scientists cannot schedule fundamental breakthroughs, and the eventual applications that arise from them may be surprises, both in form and in timing. Ordinarily, the ultimate commercial applications are entirely unforeseen when the initial, enabling discoveries are made in university laboratories. It has been forty-eight years since Watson and Crick discovered the double helix, and the enormous practical benefits of this discovery are only now beginning to be realized through new medical treatments and a whole new technology for developing pharmaceuticals. Universities, in their unending, unadulterated search to know, are uniquely situated to undertake such long-term research without worrying about its commercial application and payoff—a luxury that profit-seeking private industrial firms cannot afford.

Examples of how university-based research has yielded enormous and unanticipated benefits are abundant. My favorite story involves Professor William Bennett, who began working on the phenomenon of coherent light in the 1950s. After he came to Yale in 1961, he continued his work with the support of grants from the U.S. Department of Defense. For many years the laser was what Professor Bennett called a "solution looking for a problem." Today there are so many uses for lasers that it would be impossible to describe them all in the time that remains. Lasers are used to cut cloth, to lay out the foundations of a house, to make microchips, to pinpoint and treat brain tumors without surgery. In fact, when Professor Bennett suffered from a detached retina in 1995, the treatment he received was accomplished by using precisely the same argon ion laser that he developed at Yale in 1964.

Aside from stimulating scientific discoveries with long-term and unpredictable economic consequences, the deliberate decision to locate most fundamental research in universities rather than in government laboratories or private research institutes had another equally significant benefit. It enabled the next generation of scientists and engineers to receive its education and training from the nation's best scientists and engineers, who are required to teach as they pursue their own research. I cannot overemphasize how conducive this model of graduate education is to the creativity of the students and also to the vitality of the research enterprise.

Of course, some of these well-trained graduate students become professors after they complete their degrees and postdoctoral study, thus ensuring that the academic research engine is continually replenished with new skilled scientists. But the many who enter industrial employment after graduation take with them invaluable assets—state-of-the-art knowledge obtained by working at the frontiers of science, and experience with the most advanced research tools and equipment. They also take with them a particular way of thinking, a topic to which I turn next.

The knowledge created by the enterprise of academic science is by no means the only contribution of American universities to economic growth. By engaging students in intellectual inquiry, making them active participants in the search to know, and fostering their problem-solving abilities, universities and colleges contribute to economic growth through their teaching as well as their research. And it is not only the education of industrial scientists and engineers that has an impact on economic performance, it is the education of all those engaged in the business sector—executives, entrepreneurs, financiers, and consultants alike.

Because the pace of technological change is so rapid, many successful companies produce products or services based on technology or marketing strategies that didn't exist a decade or two ago. In such a world, knowledge of a given body of information is not enough to survive, much less thrive; business leaders must have the ability to think critically and creatively, and to draw on and adapt ideas to new environments.

The methods of undergraduate, as well as much professional, education used by America's most selective and distinguished universities and liberal arts colleges are particularly well suited to prepare students for a changing world. Unlike British universities, which require students to specialize early, America's finest research universities and liberal arts colleges are committed to the "liberal education" of undergraduates. And, of course, Yale has long been distinctive for the breadth of education that it provides to its engineering undergraduates.

A liberal education cultivates the intellect and expands the capacity to reason and to empathize. Its object is not to convey any particular content but to develop certain qualities of mind: the ability to think critically and independently, to be creative and innovative, to liberate oneself from prejudice and superstition, to sift through information, to extract what is useful and discard what is irrelevant. Just as the largest social benefits derive from scientific research that is undertaken without any focus on a commercially salient objective, so, I would argue, the largest social benefits derive from a pedagogy that seeks to enlarge the power of students to reason and think creatively without focus on mastering a particular body of knowledge.

What does this mean in practical terms? It means that, at America's best universities and colleges, education is not a one-way street. Information is not simply conveyed from faculty to students. Even as recently as the 1930s and '40s, in many college classes, professors spewed forth information in lectures and students copiously took notes, memorized them, and then "recited" them back to the professor when called upon in class. Today students cannot rely on a good memory to succeed in college. Although lectures are still used in many courses, students are no longer encouraged to recite back what they hear in class or read in a textbook. Instead, students are encouraged to think for themselves—to offer their own opinions and interpretations in seminars and discussion sections.

Professors also encourage critical thinking by the form of writing assignments they require and by the kind of examination questions they ask. In the mid-1980s, while he was president of Harvard, Derek Bok studied the examinations given there in various subjects since 1900. He found that, at the beginning of the century, nearly all of exam questions "sought to have students repeat particular facts, describe the opinions of others, or relate fixed sequences of events. . . . The emphasis was chiefly on memory."[1] As the century progressed, the nature of exams changed in a way that increasingly "emphasized analysis rather than memory or description." By 1960, according to Bok, "half of the questions in the humanities and social sciences called upon students to discuss complex problems from more than one perspective."[2] As Bok's survey shows, students today are expected to take from their courses not just facts, figures, and widely accepted theories, but a way of thinking—the ability to use facts and figures to support an argument and to confront one theory with another through critical analysis.

The distinctive emphasis on critical thinking produces graduates who are intellectually flexible and open to new ideas, graduates equipped with curiosity and the capacity to adapt to ever-changing work environments, graduates who can convert recently discovered knowledge into new products and services. By producing thoughtful and engaged leaders capable of thriving in the new age of information technology, American higher education prepares the nation for the

1. Derek Bok, *Higher Learning* (Cambridge, Mass.: Harvard University Press, 1986), pp. 48–49.
2. Bok, *Higher Learning, p.* 49.

challenges that we can't even imagine today, challenges upon which continued growth and prosperity depends.

There is doubtless some irony in all of this. For the most part, universities conduct scientific research without concern for potential commercial application, and liberal education seeks not to train business and professional men and women but to produce inquisitive, thinking, creative citizens. Still, the research and teaching done in American universities have a profound and hugely positive effect on practical affairs.

Both the organization of scientific research and the pedagogical strategies used in our finest universities and colleges contribute mightily to America's technological leadership and ultimately to national and worldwide economic growth.

Recognition of this distinctive contribution of U.S. universities should not encourage complacency. To the contrary, we must keep extending the frontiers of science and improving the efficacy of our pedagogy. We do not take our responsibilities lightly. We know that in no small measure the fate of our students, the nation, and the global economy depends on us.

Universities as Urban Citizens

The recent Summit for America's Future highlighted the importance of engaging the voluntary efforts of individual citizens to reclaim the nation's dream of opportunity for all. Although the Philadelphia convocation also encouraged the involvement of business corporations in curing society's ills, little was said about another potent force for community revitalization that is taking root and flourishing throughout the nation. I refer to the growing contributions of colleges and universities to economic and human development in America's cities.

The emergence of colleges and universities as significant institutional citizens is no accident. As manufacturing enterprises have fled our cities, educational institutions, and their associated medical centers, have become the principal employers in urban America. New Haven was a hub of manufacturing as recently as thirty-five years ago, but Yale is now the city's largest employer, nine times larger than the largest manufacturer. A similar pattern has emerged across the country. The University of Alabama is the largest employer in Birmingham, once a major steel center. Brigham Young is the largest employer in Provo, as is Johns Hopkins in Baltimore. The three largest private employers in Philadelphia are the University of Pennsylvania, Temple University, and Thomas Jefferson University. In Cambridge, Massachusetts, employment by colleges and universities exceeds 22 percent of the total work force.

An opinion column in the *Boston Globe*, April 29, 1997

Institutions of higher education are especially well suited to contribute to the betterment of their urban surroundings, because faculty, students, staff, and alumni possess considerable expertise. There is also a natural harmony of interests. Just as universities desire healthy cities to make themselves more attractive to prospective students and faculty, city leaders should recognize that healthy universities, and their affiliated medical centers, provide a strong, stable base of urban employment that is increasingly the principal engine of urban economic growth.

Many of our urban colleges and universities have long and distinguished traditions of encouraging student and faculty volunteerism. At Yale, half of our undergraduates and 90 percent of our medical students participate in community service. Students in Yale College help young children learn to read. Music School students and faculty work with their counterparts at a nearby high school. Students from the School of Architecture assist in neighborhood planning efforts and housing rehabilitation. Students in the School of Forestry and Environmental Studies work to improve our parks and neighborhood safety, and law students have an active program of legal assistance.

These voluntary efforts are valuable and important, and some are long-standing. A more recent development is the recognition by colleges and universities that we have a responsibility that goes beyond encouraging individual volunteerism; we must participate as *institutional* citizens in the betterment of our communities. All around the country, colleges and universities are beginning to form partnerships with their neighbors—working together with city government, business leaders, clergy, and neighborhood organizations on issues of economic development, neighborhood revitalization, and human development.

In the area of economic development, for example, Yale has helped to persuade the business community to join us in making supplemental payments to support a special services district to enhance the safety and cleanliness of downtown New Haven. We also initiated a "Buy in New Haven" program to encourage decentralized purchasers around the campus to give preference to local vendors for routinely purchased supplies and services. In several cases we have helped local businesses develop the capacity to meet our procurement standards, and we also helped another business to relocate in the city. In three years purchases by Yale in New Haven increased by 23 percent.

We have also sought to promote home ownership within the city. We created the New Haven Home Buyer Program for all full-time Yale employees in 1994, providing a cash benefit of $20,000, payable over ten years, to those who purchase homes in the city. In the first three years of the program, 262 employees have participated. Yale's $5.3 million commitment to date has yielded more than $28 million in home sales in New Haven, and it has stabilized and strengthened a distressed housing market in the city's largest middle-class neighborhoods. In the current, second phase of the program, we have increased the subsidy and restricted it to a targeted set of neighborhoods most in need of home ownership. In these neighborhoods, more than 90 percent of the participating employees are first-time homebuyers.[1]

Many educational institutions lack the resources to support an initiative on the scale of our Home Buyer Program, but all colleges and universities have people skilled in grant-writing and program development. In Worcester, Massachusetts, for example, Clark University faculty and staff have brought these skills to a partnership with municipal government and a neighborhood association to secure resources for revitalization efforts planned by local residents. Their efforts helped the partnership secure a $2.4 million grant from the Department of Housing and Urban Development. The funds will establish a multi-function community center, acquire and renovate blighted and abandoned housing, and create a center for entrepreneurial development.

The third focus of institutional involvement is human development, especially education. A major component of Trinity College's vigorous partnership with business and government in Hartford is

1. By mid-2002, more than 500 Yale employees had participated in the Home Buyers Program.

the establishment of a community of learning in the neighborhood that surrounds the campus. The Trinity-Hartford collaboration will direct efforts toward supporting a Montessori-style magnet elementary school, a neighborhood middle school, and an inter-district high school science and math resource center.

Similarly, Marquette University's College of Engineering supports science teaching in the Milwaukee Public Schools, and faculty in the College of Arts and Sciences help design and implement innovations in the teaching of mathematics. And Harvard University has a long and distinguished record of collaboration with schools in Cambridge and Boston. In addition to the many contributions of the Graduate School of Education, the Kennedy School has an active partnership with Graham and Parks School, and the Business School works closely with Taft Middle School.

Clark, Marquette, Trinity, Harvard, and Yale are only some of the many colleges and universities around the country that are beginning to assume responsibility as leading institutional citizens in their communities. Washington University in St. Louis, Johns Hopkins in Baltimore, and the University of Pennsylvania in West Philadelphia, among others, have undertaken notable initiatives. Although these efforts can be justified on the purely pragmatic grounds that universities require a safe and attractive environment, they also flow naturally from the mission and purpose of any institution of higher education.

On our campuses we are devoted to the full development of human potential, and we provide extraordinary support to facilitate such development in our students and faculty. Outside our walls, many of our neighbors live in conditions that do not provide sufficient opportunity for the realization of their potential. To ensure the health of our democracy, we must help provide those without privilege access to such opportunity and the knowledge to make use of it.

Our responsibility as institutions of higher education thus transcends mere pragmatism. We must help our cities become what we hope our campuses are—places where human potential can be fully realized.

The Global University

This year marks the three hundredth anniversary of the found- ing of Yale University. We have chosen to mark this historic oc- casion by bringing a delegation of faculty, administrators, and one of our trustees to China.

Understanding China and developing relationships with its people and institutions are of great importance to us. I say this not only because of the size of your population, your significant role in world politics, and the immense potential of your rapidly growing economy. For a university such as Yale, which aspires to be among the greatest in the world, China is also important for the achievements of its ancient and continuous civilization, which is an unending source of learning and enlightenment for scholars who seek comprehensive understanding of the human condition.

Yale's mission and the scope of its influence have evolved grad- ually over the past three centuries from a local to a regional to a national institution. The university has made a dramatic mark on American society by educating leaders in every field of endeavor. Four of the last six presidents of the United States have Yale degrees; 55 of our graduates have served in the president's Cabinet, and 533 have served in the U.S. Congress. Yale graduates have led many of Amer- ica's best-known business organizations—Coca-Cola and Procter and Gamble, Time Magazine and Federal Express, Goldman Sachs

Based on a speech delivered at Peking University, May 7, 2001 and J.P. Morgan, IBM and Real Networks. And Yale graduates served as the first presidents of Princeton, Columbia, Cornell, and Johns Hopkins Universities, the University of Chicago, and the Universities of Georgia, Mississippi, Missouri, Wisconsin, and California.

Yale has also been an innovator in higher education within the United States. We were the first American university to establish a program in public health, a school of nursing, a school of fine art, and a school of forestry. We were the first to have an art museum, the first to appoint a professor of science, and the first to grant a Ph.D.

As Yale enters its fourth century, our goal is to become a truly global university—educating leaders and advancing the frontiers of knowledge not simply for the United States, but for the entire world.

The globalization of the university is in part an evolutionary development. Yale has drawn students from outside the United States for nearly two centuries, and international issues have been represented in its curriculum for the past hundred years and more. But creating the global university is also a revolutionary development—signaling distinct changes in the substance of teaching and research, the demographic characteristics of students, the scope and breadth of external collaborations, and the engagement of the university with new audiences. Let me discuss in turn each of these aspects of the global university.

Teaching and Research

When I speak of becoming a global university, I envision a curriculum and a research agenda permeated by awareness that political, economic, social, and cultural phenomena in any part of the world can no longer be fully understood in isolation. The revolution in communications technology has brought the world closer together and changed the way we think about it.

The term globalization is much used these days, although we have yet to disentangle entirely its several meanings. In one sense globalization refers to economic interdependence. The movement of capital across national borders is now instantaneous, and the movement of products, people, and, unfortunately, pollution is freer and faster than ever before. These facts make comprehensive governance of the economy impossible at the level of the nation-state. International institutions are needed to regulate trade, capital flows, and environmental degradation. Isolation is not an option.

In another sense globalization refers to the instantaneous transmission of ideas and images. Cross-cultural influences have always been with us, but today they are more powerful because of their immediacy. Because we access the same web sites, radio broadcasts, and television programs, many fear a growing homogenization of cultures and values. The incipiency of a common global culture has precipitated, in many parts of the world, a defensive reaction to protect local values, heightening tensions among neighboring ethnic, religious, and cultural groups.

Yale is well prepared to meet the challenge of understanding these developments. We teach fifty-two languages, offer over six hundred courses on international topics, and we sponsor research and teaching programs focused on each of the world's major regions.

A global university can be built upon this strong foundation, but the superstructure must encompass new forms as well as old. Because the world's problems cannot be neatly compartmentalized into traditional academic categories, we are creating under the auspices of the Yale Center for International and Area Studies a set of special professorships for scholars whose work on international subjects extends beyond the boundaries of a single academic discipline. And, as a major initiative of our tercentennial year, we have announced the establishment of a new Yale Center for the Study of Globalization. The center will host visiting scholars and practitioners, support research, and foster the development of new teaching materials concerning globalization. In addition to embracing these traditional functions, the new center will develop a professionally edited web site and a web-based journal of opinion. It will also promote dialogue among representatives of opposing parties involved in regional or global conflict.

Students

Just as building a global university requires us to expand our curriculum and refocus our research, it also requires us to ask whom are we educating and for what purpose. Yale educated the first Chinese to graduate from any American university. Yung Wing came to Yale in 1850 from Guandong province, and when he returned to China after graduation he became an advocate for improving technical education in his homeland. He organized the Chinese Educational Mission in 1872, which sent over one hundred young Chinese men to study in preparatory schools and then to enroll in colleges throughout New England. Over twenty of these young scholars came to Yale, among them Zhan Tianyou, who later became known as the Father of China's Railroads.

Today, more than 30 percent of Yale's Ph.D. students are neither citizens nor permanent residents of the United States. Within the past six years we have increased the representation of international students in our undergraduate college from 4 to nearly 8 percent.

This representation of international students constitutes a strong foundation, but a global university must have aspirations beyond mere numbers. We have for some years offered international graduate students the same financial aid awards that we extend to U.S. citizens. But we want to be certain that we are also attracting the very best undergraduate students from around the world. To this end we recently announced that from now on we will admit international students to Yale College on exactly the same basis as we admit U.S. citizens. That is, we will admit students without regard to their ability to pay and offer the full financial assistance that they need to attend. We hope and expect that this new policy will have a profound effect on our ability to attract undergraduates from many countries around the world where families are typically unable to pay the full cost of a Yale education.

We not only provide generous financial aid for full-time students in residence at Yale, we also intend to increase the resources available for overseas study and exchange visits. We are expanding the very successful Fox International Fellowship Program, which currently sponsors graduate student exchange visits with six major universities around the world—Cambridge University, the Free University of Berlin, l'Institut d'études politiques de Paris, Moscow State University, Tokyo University, and Fudan University.

In addition to these various programs supporting international students at Yale, overseas study opportunities for Yale students, and exchange visits, we have marked our Tercentennial by launching an ambitious and innovative effort to provide a touchstone experience for emerging leaders from around the world. Each year the new Yale World Fellows Program will recruit a small group of emerging leaders representing all sectors of society and all regions of the world. The Fellows will spend an intensive twelve-week period at Yale studying global problems under the tutelage of our most distinguished professors. The program will encourage the Fellows to develop new skills and contacts that will serve them and their countries on their return home. By holding regular reunions of all the Fellows, we would hope to create a network of world leaders who can draw on one another's strengths as their careers develop.

International Collaborations

I have discussed how the creation of a global university will affect on-campus teaching and research, as well as the number and type of students we educate and the international experiences we provide for them. But an equally powerful impetus for change will come from increased opportunities to collaborate with other institutions.

Partnership in education and research is not a new concept. Indeed, the idea has long been employed successfully by the Yale-China Association, whose one hundredth anniversary we are celebrating in conjunction with the University's Tercentennial. During its first half century Yale-China's work was concentrated principally in Changsha and Wuhan, where it helped to found the Yali Middle School, the Hsiang-Ya Hospital, Medical College, and Nursing School, and Hua-chung University. Today, four Yale College graduates teach English each year at the Yali School, and the Yale School of Nursing has several active collaborations with Hunan Medical University, including a "train-the-trainer" program that teaches Chinese nurses how to teach other nurses to prevent the transmission of blood-borne pathogens.

In all, Yale has more than twenty active collaborations with Chinese universities, health care organizations, and government agencies. Among these is a multifaceted partnership with the Union School of Public Health in Beijing to make significant changes in public health education, as well as several research and training programs in the area of forest management and natural resource sustainability.

Two new and very significant collaborative projects will be officially launched this week during our visit to Beijing. Here at Peking University we will be officially dedicating today a recently established research partnership in the area of plant genomics and agricultural biotechnology. This is a fully collaborative project involving exchange visits of scientists from both Yale and Peking Universities as they work together to study the basic biology of plant systems with potential relevance to crop improvement in both China and the United States.

Tomorrow we will be announcing the creation of the China Law Center, a collaboration of the Yale Law School, several Chinese law schools and institutes, the State Council Office of Legislative Affairs, and the Legislative Affairs Commission of the Standing Committee of the National People's Congress. The new center, led by Professor Paul Gewirtz, has formed project teams consisting of leading legal scholars, judges, other government officials, and practicing lawyers from both China and the United States. Together they will address the issues of judicial reform, administrative law, and legal education.

These collaborations exemplify the future of scholarship and service in the global university. They permit scholars and scientists to share expertise in the pursuit of new knowledge and in the application of that knowledge to improving material and social conditions. They will flourish best if scholars are free to ask questions, collect information, and conduct research. We are proud to be deeply engaged in so many partnerships here in China, and we look forward to expanding the scope of cooperative activity in the future.

New Audiences

The same advances in communications technology that have created the phenomenon we call globalization offer substantial opportunities for the global university to expand its educational mission. The Yale web site already contains many audio and video reproductions of lectures and conferences that have recently taken place on our campus, but we have only begun to tap the potential of the Internet to provide valuable on-line learning experiences for students around the world.

To this end, Yale has recently joined with Oxford and Stanford Universities in an alliance to develop on-line educational materials. Our approach is deliberately experimental. Some of our offerings will approximate conventional university "courses" in the arts and sciences, but we will also experiment with offerings of different duration and format. We will test some of these offerings with audiences consisting principally of the alumni of our three universities, but eventually we hope to offer the best of what we develop to students and adult learners worldwide.

In closing, I thank you for permitting me this opportunity to address you today. I hope that I have given you reason to reflect upon the impact of globalization on teaching and research, the students we educate, the partnerships we enter, and the audiences we will come to embrace. As Yale begins its fourth century, we are rising to the challenge of becoming a global university. We invite Peking University, our host and partner, and a great center of teaching and learning, to join us in this important effort.

The Graduate's Role in Society

Education for Self and
for Others

We celebrate this weekend a commencement, a beginning, the beginning of your lives as independent, educated citizens of this nation and the world. This celebration marks also an end, the end of your bright college years—so abounding with activity, so ripe with experiment, so full of hope. We the faculty celebrate with you as we loose you on the wider world—confident of your success and hopeful that your newly acquired knowledge and critical powers will be directed toward finding answers that have eluded us.

Yale tradition permits me this one last word, this one last opportunity to teach. I shall draw upon a tradition of teaching far older than Yale's, a tradition that speaks powerfully to the choices before you at this moment. The Talmud is a compendium of oral law reduced to writing by rabbis some time around the third century A.D. It consists of laws, or teachings (*mishnah*), and a related set of rabbinical commentaries (*gemara*). These commentaries are extraordinary examples of legal and literary interpretation. The methods of the commentators survive in the work of legal scholars and literary critics to this day.

Baccalaureate Address, May 22, 1994

Ten years ago, in the Baccalaureate Address to the Yale Class of 1984, my predecessor, A. Bartlett Giamatti, commented on a passage drawn from a section of the Talmud known as the *Pirke Avot,* "the sayings of the ancestors." Unlike the rest of the Talmud, the *Pirke Avot* is not a compendium of obligatory laws or prescriptions for ritual observance. It is instead a set of stories and maxims, the ethical teachings of the rabbis who lived in the period from perhaps 300 B.C. to A.D. 200. Today, I shall take inspiration from the ethical teachings of Hillel, a Babylonian rabbi who lived and taught in Jerusalem just before the time of Jesus.

The *Pirke Avot* records: "[Hillel] used to say: 'If I am not for myself, who will be for me? If I am for myself alone, what am I? And if not now, when?' "

"If I am not for myself, who will be for me?" Hillel's observation arises in the context of a discussion of self-improvement through study. Each of you has learned that the development of your intellectual capabilities (not to mention your aesthetic, emotional, and spiritual capabilities) requires effort that only you can apply. It is true that the Yale environment has provided you with extraordinarily abundant resources to facilitate learning: a distinguished and engaged faculty, library and museum collections that are among the finest available to students anywhere, laboratories and computing resources, a unique residential college system, myriad extracurricular activities, athletic and cultural events for both participant and observer. But your education has not merely been laid before you; you have worked hard to acquire it—in the classroom, on the playing fields, in extracurricular activities, in the community. You have learned to be for yourselves. You may have benefited from the support and encouragement of others, but they were and will be for you only to the extent that you responded to their support and encouragement by becoming independent, autonomous persons.

Two millennia after Hillel, I would suggest that being "for oneself" is still the principal object of study and reflection. Though discussion of what it means to be an educated person usually focuses on the content of one's course of study, the essence of a liberal education is to develop the freedom to think critically and independently, to cultivate one's mind to its fullest potential. What you have learned at Yale—the specific knowledge you have worked hard to acquire—matters. What matters more is that you have learned how to learn.

This is something you should not easily surrender. Tempting as it may be to conform to prevailing orthodoxies, resist them. Guide your daily lives by the same rigorous standards of critical inquiry that have been demanded of you in the classroom. Question every assumption and every argument, make them your own, be for yourself. Some of the commentators on Hillel observe that his teaching echoes Deuteronomy (30:15): "See I have set before thee this day life and good, and death and evil. . . . Choose life, therefore . . ." Choose, therefore, to keep alive your precious power of independent, open-minded, critical inquiry.

Hillel reminds us that self-improvement through study is not enough: "If I am for myself alone, what am I?" Our commitment to a life of learning must not diminish, it must indeed reinforce, our commitment to those around us. The rabbinical commentators provide various interpretations of this teaching. Some suggest that the learned, those who study the divine law, are obliged to transmit their learning, to teach and to encourage in others the habit of study and a disciplined approach to self-development. Other commentators find in Hillel's question the suggestion of a more general ethical imperative to use one's learning, one's critical powers, in the service of others.

Both these interpretations—that we are obliged to teach and to serve—resonate with the history of this great university. Yale has been a mother of great teachers. Our graduates have taught with distinction at all levels, sharing the benefits of their Yale education with students in New England schools and colleges in the eighteenth century, across the United States in the nineteenth century, around the world in the twentieth. At this time of year, blue gowns are in abundance, not only here at Yale but in commencement processions throughout the land.

Most of you will not choose teaching as a vocation, but all of you will teach—in the workplace, in the community, in the family. Take this opportunity seriously. Others have much to gain from what you will make of your Yale education. Nurture in others what Yale has encouraged you to develop for yourselves—the capacity for rigorous analysis, for critical reflection, for independent thought.

Hillel's teaching can also be interpreted as a call to service. If we are for ourselves alone, we overlook and neglect the needs and aspirations of others. There is a famous story about the student who came to Hillel seeking conversion to Judaism, but only on the condition that Hillel would teach him the entire divine law, the entire Torah, while the student stood on one foot. Hillel replied with his distinctive formulation of the Golden Rule: "What is hateful to you, do not do to another. That is the whole Torah, the rest is commentary. Go and learn!"

The idea that a Yale education should be used in the service of others is as old as the university itself. Our charter of 1701 describes Yale, then called the Collegiate School, as a place "wherein Youth . . . may be fitted for Publick employment both in Church and Civil State." For nearly three centuries Yale has fulfilled this founding mission, supplying leaders to serve the nation and the world. In politics, religion, business, law, medicine, and the arts, as well as in education, Yale alumni have served the public with distinction. Countless Yale graduates have served their communities—not only in their primary careers, but also through selfless involvement with voluntary associations of all kinds.

Heavy though the burden may seem, you will be among the leaders of your generation. The world you will serve presents you with more than a few challenges: the resurgence of nationalism and ethnic struggle around the globe, the desperate condition of the inner-city poor here in this country, the degradation of our environment. You bring to these challenges more than the mere enthusiasm of youth. You bring the ability to see these problems in a new light, to think them through again, using the critical intelligence that you have developed for yourselves. Rise to these challenges; be not for yourselves alone.

Your experience here at Yale encourages us. Many, perhaps most of you, have found time, despite the demands of a rigorous academic program, for a serious commitment to community service. The recent dramatic increase in the number of Yale students engaged in community service gives hope, not only for the city of New Haven whose residents have benefited from your involvement, but for the communities in which you will live and for the wider world whose problems you must not shun.

"And if not now, when?" In interpreting this last of Hillel's questions, I have little to add to the commentaries of the rabbis. Maimonides, a twelfth-century philosopher, said: "If now, in the days of my youth, I do not acquire good qualities, when shall I acquire them?" The good qualities to which he refers are the habits of study as a means to self-improvement and service. A thirteenth-century commentator, Rabbi Jonah, adds: "Let no one say, 'Today, I am busy with my work; tomorrow I will turn to the task of perfecting myself.' Perchance the opportunity will not present itself. And even if it does, that particular day has vanished utterly . . . it can never be recovered."

Self-improvement and service to others are tasks that require more than a lifetime, but they must be undertaken. Let me recall to you the teaching of Rabbi Tarphon, the second-century scholar who inspired Bart Giamatti a decade ago and who reminds us of these obligations: "You are not required to complete the work, but neither are you free to desist from it."

Women and men of the Class of 1994: The challenges you face are daunting, but you are magnificently prepared for them. Your Yale education has given you gifts that few possess. Use them well. Make your own lives full of continued study, reflection, and learning, and, through teaching and service, make better the lives of others.

On Controversy

We gather here as one community to celebrate your commencement, to rejoice in your accomplishments. It is a time for reflection—a time to give thanks for the devotion of your teachers, for the lessons you have learned, for the bonds you have formed with classmates, for the beauty of this place.

It may seem contrary to the spirit of the occasion, but I would like to speak to you about controversy—its inevitability in a free society, its occasional unpleasantness, and, ultimately, its value. We have had a substantial measure of controversy on our campus this past year.[1] It would seem appropriate to reflect on what we have learned.

James Madison describes the inevitability of controversy in public life in *The Federalist Papers:* "The latent causes of faction are . . . sown in the nature of man. . . . A zeal for different opinions . . . [has] divided mankind into parties, inflamed them with mutual animosity, and rendered them much more to vex and oppress each other than to co-operate for their common good."[2]

Madison points out that it is among the tasks of government to regulate the competing interests that give rise to controversy, though he sees no realistic means of suppressing it. He writes, "There are two methods of curing the mischiefs of faction: the one, by destroying the

Baccalaureate Address, May 26, 1996

1. During the spring semester of 1996, each of the university's two largest labor unions had engaged in a monthlong strike.
2. James Madison, *The Federalist Papers,* no. 10 (London: Penguin, 1987), p. 124.

liberty that is essential to its existence; the other, by giving to every citizen the same opinions, the same passions, and the same interests."[3]

Let us pause over this a moment. Madison's first point is that suppressing freedom of expression can stifle controversy, but this would be an unacceptable solution. More interesting is the second method of eliminating controversy—giving every citizen the same opinions. Madison claims this is "impracticable" for two reasons: First, "as long as the reason of man continues fallible, and he is at liberty to exercise it, different opinions will be formed." Second, "The diversity in the faculties of men . . . is not less an insuperable obstacle to a uniformity of interests."

Thus, Madison believes that the harmonization of competing values and interests is merely impracticable, not impossible. If all men were endowed with equal and adequate critical faculties, all would reason their way to common conclusions. A uniformity of values and interests would emerge.

The belief that all competing values can be harmonized, that all interests can be finally reconciled, is a common feature of Platonic, Judeo-Christian, Enlightenment, and Marxist thought, though it is expressed in very different forms. As Sir Isaiah Berlin, the distinguished historian of ideas and political philosopher, explains, three common threads run through these systems of belief. First, all genuine questions have one and only one true answer. Second, there is a dependable path to the discovery of these truths—which in different systems of belief involves a different combination of reason, faith, and divine intervention. Third, the answers to all genuine questions are compatible with one another and form a single whole, for it is assumed that one truth cannot be inconsistent with another.[4]

Berlin argues that conflict among values is inevitable for reasons

3. Ibid., p. 123.
4. Isaiah Berlin, "The Pursuit of the Ideal," in Berlin, *The Crooked Timber of Humanity* (New York: Knopf, 1991), pp. 5–6. See also Berlin, "The Decline of Utopian Ideas in the West," in *Crooked Timber,* pp. 24–25.

different from those advanced by Madison. The goals of liberty and equality, justice and mercy—to give just two examples of legitimate personal and societal objectives—cannot be completely reconciled. Reason cannot lead us to a unitary solution that realizes all the aspirations of humanity; many legitimate goals cannot be achieved simultaneously. Choices must be made; compromises among values must be found. There is no single answer to the question of how much liberty should be sacrificed in the name of equality, or how much justice should be tempered with mercy. Cultures will reach different conclusions about how to balance these objectives, as will individuals within a culture such as our own.

I mentioned at the outset that controversy is not only inevitable, it can be unpleasant. As Madison points out, controversies in the public arena can inflame factions with mutual animosity, kindle unfriendly passions, and excite violent conflict. As Berlin argues, the single-minded pursuit of a unitary vision can blind an individual or group to the legitimacy of competing values and thus eliminate the possibility of compromise. In the extreme, single-mindedness becomes narrow-mindedness: it leads to the suppression of dissenting views, to the totalitarian denial of life and liberty.

In a free society, we seek to counter the tendency for controversy to degenerate by establishing rules and observing customs that preserve civility. In this university we have a strong tradition of tolerating controversy. Free expression is protected, even if the speaker's words are bitter, disrespectful, insensitive, or hurtful. Those who utter offending words are not punished; instead, those who interfere with the rights of speakers to speak are subject to discipline. These rules combine to produce an atmosphere of free and open debate, a climate in which the answer to a false argument or a hurtful argument is not the suppression of speech but more speech; argument is met with counterargument.

The controversy on our campus this past year has for the most part honored these rules of civility. Passions have been inflamed, and, at times, rhetoric has been shrill. Demonstrably false claims have been trumpeted as truths. This has been uncomfortable, even disturbing, but each side has had ample opportunity to make its case.

If conflict among legitimate values is inevitable, how should we conduct ourselves? If Berlin is right, we must not only compromise with one another, but each of us must privately balance the competing claims of legitimate yet ultimately irreconcilable values. Berlin often cites the great philosopher Immanuel Kant, who said, "Out of the crooked timber of humanity, nothing straight was ever built."[5]

We cannot build a perfect life or a perfect world. But this should not deter us from building a better life or a better world. To recognize that values ultimately clash is not to deny the possibility of ethical conduct. By a thoughtful, well-reasoned assessment of competing claims, one can chart a highly principled, if not an ideal, course of action.

Let us take Abraham Lincoln as an example. David Donald's new biography makes clear the sense in which Lincoln was both a pragmatist and a man of principle.[6] He was not inalterably committed to a single, unchanging vision that directed all his actions. He entered his presidency driven by the objective of preserving the Union. Gradually, by a combination of external circumstances and the growth of his own self-confidence, he came to grasp that bringing an end to slavery was a practical possibility. Thus, he allowed another objective—that all men are created equal—to become a guiding principle.

Lincoln's principled pragmatism stands in stark contrast to behavior driven by a single, all-embracing vision. Among the fragments of writing left by the Greek poet Archilochus, Isaiah Berlin found vivid expression for this opposition: "The fox knows many things, but the hedgehog knows one big thing." Lincoln did not, in Berlin's words, "relate everything to a single central mission," a "single, uni-

5. Isaiah Berlin, *Two Concepts of Liberty* (Oxford: Clarendon, 1958), p. 56; Berlin, "Pursuit of the Ideal," pp. 18–19; "Decline of Utopian Ideas," p. 48.
6. David Donald, *Lincoln* (New York: Simon and Schuster, 1995).

versal organizing principle in terms of which alone all that [he was] and [said] has significance." Like the fox, Lincoln "seized upon the essence of a vast variety of objects for what they are in themselves, without . . . seeking to fit them into . . . any one unchanging, all-embracing . . . sometimes self-contradictory and incomplete, at times fanatical, unitary inner vision."[7]

Now some of you who graduate this weekend may be hedgehogs, and to you I would say: beware the excesses of the true believer. Use the tools of critical inquiry you have acquired here at Yale to remind yourselves that the end you seek—however worthwhile in itself—does not always, does not often, and perhaps does not ever, justify means that are intolerant and inhumane.

To those of you who are foxes, I would say: prepare yourselves to tolerate ambiguity, to accept the fact that conflict among values is inescapable. Your lives and the world you live in are imperfect, but your Yale education has prepared you for them. You have learned to think clearly and independently, to disentangle difficult ideas, to weigh and balance competing claims as you shape your own lives.

Women and men of the Class of 1996, hedgehogs and foxes alike: I hope that you will never be overwhelmed by controversy, but that you will not avoid it altogether. Use the powers that you have developed here to learn from the struggle with competing ideas and values. Though you may not build Jerusalem, may you never cease to improve yourselves and the world around you.

7. Isaiah Berlin, *The Hedgehog and the Fox* (London: Weidenfeld and Nicolson, 1953), pp. 1–2.

Taking the Next Step

We began together. We met here, in this grand hall, sweltering in the heat of late summer. A thunderstorm kept you and your parents from strolling down Hillhouse Avenue to a garden reception. We scrambled instead to receive you in Commons, where, duped by a campus humor magazine to believe you were participating in an ancient tradition, you each handed me a blue bead.

You were the first class that Dean Brodhead and I had the pleasure of greeting, and you are the first class that we have watched, with much admiration, through four years. And now, your beads returned, you sit before us again.

It is natural to think of this occasion as an ending. This weekend you will look back with mixed emotions—pride in your accomplishments, regret for opportunities not seized, joy for the friends you have made, and sadness in leaving them. But even as you are looking back, let me take this moment to look forward. For it is not by accident that this ending, this completion of four intense and rewarding years, is called a commencement, a beginning. It is a beginning, the beginning of your lives as independent, educated citizens of this nation and the world.

To graduate is, quite literally, to take a step. Some of you are eager to take that step, to march straight ahead with a clear sense of purpose and direction. But most of you are still asking yourselves

Baccalaureate Address, May 25, 1997

119

anxiously where the next step leads. This division within your ranks—between those who have clarity about a future course and those who do not—is to be expected. The discovery of one's true calling may come early. More often it comes late, and it may come more than once in a lifetime.

We are fortunate that many of our greatest writers have left behind reflections on the stage of life that now lies ahead of you. It is instructive, and reassuring, to compare the experience of two of the greatest English poets. They lived in different times and in a different place from you, and they had exceptional gifts. But you will recognize something familiar in the story of how each came to choose a life's course. William Wordsworth had a clear direction by the summer of 1788, after only one year at Cambridge. By contrast, John Milton, whom Harold Bloom calls "still the morning and evening star" of poetry in the English language, considered himself a late bloomer.[1] It was years after his graduation in 1629 before he began to show evidence of his genius.

Paradoxically, it was Wordsworth who was the more alienated from the academic side of the undergraduate experience. In his autobiographical poem *The Prelude*, he tells us of his distaste for lectures, examinations, and competition among his fellow students. More in touch with nature than with his studies, Wordsworth spent much of his first year at Cambridge in solitary reflection and the rest enjoying the company of his friends. He had frequent melancholy, fears about his future livelihood,

> And, more than all, a strangeness in my mind,
> A feeling that I was not for that hour,
> Nor for that place.[2]

---

1. Harold Bloom, *Ruin the Sacred Truths* (Cambridge, Mass.: Harvard University Press, 1989), p. 113.
2. William Wordsworth, *The Prelude* (Text of 1805), edited by Ernest De Selincourt (London: Oxford University Press, revised impression, 1960), Book III, Lines 79–81.

That summer, back in his beloved Lake District, his epiphany came. In *The Prelude* he recalls walking home at dawn after a night of "dancing, gaiety, and mirth":

> Magnificent
> The morning was, a memorable pomp,
> More glorious than I ever had beheld.
> The Sea was laughing at a distance; all
> The solid Mountains were as bright as clouds,
> Grain-tinctured, drench'd in empyrean light;
> And, in the meadows and the lower grounds,
> Was all the sweetness of a common dawn,
> Dews, vapours, and the melody of birds,
> And Labourers going forth into the fields.
> —Ah! I need say, dear Friend, that to the brim
> My heart was full; I made no vows, but vows
> Were then made for me; bond unknown to me
> Was given, that I should be, else sinning greatly,
> A dedicated Spirit. On I walk'd
> In blessedness, which even yet remains.[3]

From that moment, Wordsworth knew his calling. Looking back, fifteen years later, he wrote of his last two years at Cambridge:

> The Poet's soul was with me at that time,
> Sweet meditations, the still overflow
> Of happiness and truth. A thousand hopes
> Were mine, a thousand tender dreams . . .
>
> Those were the days
> Which also first encourag'd me to trust
> With firmness, hitherto but lightly touch'd
> With such a daring thought, that I might leave

---

3. Ibid., Book IV, Lines 330–345.

> Some monument behind me which pure hearts
> Should reverence.[4]

Wordsworth thus emerged from Cambridge with a clear calling and the very great ambition to leave a monument behind. I cite this example not to intimidate you but rather to inspire those of you whose hopes and dreams have already taken specific shape. To you I would say: you can achieve what you have imagined, for you are better prepared than you think. In the company of so many talented classmates and teachers you may seem to yourself just another person of ordinary capability. But what you miss, and what your teachers see more clearly and delight in, is that every one of you has the capacity to make a difference in the world.

For those of you who are still formulating your hopes and dreams, the example of Milton serves better. Unlike Wordsworth, Milton loved his studies from the beginning, perhaps to a fault, because he did little else but study. He published only one poem before his thirty-sixth birthday, a tribute to Shakespeare. His lines reveal how heavily the greatness of his poetic precursor weighed upon him:

> each heart
> Hath from the leaves of thy unvalued book,
> Those Delphic lines with deep impression took,
> Then thou our fancy of itself bereaving,
> Dost make us marble with too much conceiving.[5]

Or, in other words, Shakespeare's poetry was so great, its impression so profound, that it turns Milton to marble, leaving his imagination to mourn its own loss.

Milton remained at Cambridge for three years beyond his first degree. After returning home to continue his studies at age twenty-four, he felt obliged to defend his "tardy moving" in a letter to a

4. Ibid., Book VI, Lines 55–69.
5. John Milton, "On Shakespeare. 1630," in *John Milton,* edited by Stephen Orgel and Jonathan Goldberg (Oxford: Oxford University Press, 1991), p. 20.

friend who had admonished him "that the hours of the night pass on." Milton acknowledged that his life was "as yet obscure and unserviceable to mankind," and he wrote "Yet that you may see that I am somewhat suspicious of myself, and do take notice of a certain belatedness in me, I am the bolder to send you some of my nightward thoughts."[6] The beautiful sonnet that followed, published twelve years later, captures in its opening lines a sentiment that may haunt some of you.

> How soon hath time the subtle thief of youth,
> Stol'n on his wing my three and twentieth year.
> My hasting days fly on with full career,
> But my late spring no bud or blossom shew'th.[7]

Despite the pathos of these lines, Milton did not regard his "belatedness" as a failure. The sonnet continues:

> Perhaps my semblance might deceive the truth,
> That I to manhood am arrived so near,
> And inward ripeness doth much less appear,
> That some more timely-happy spirits endueth.[8]

Without bud or blossom to show, Milton was nonetheless confident of his own "inward ripeness." It took him another decade to conceive of a drama on the Fall of Man; it was still another twenty-five years before *Paradise Lost,* transformed into an epic, was published. Even then, Milton reminds us of his late development when he writes in Book IX:

> Since first this subject for heroic song
> Pleas'd me long choosing, and beginning late.[9]

6. John Milton, "Letter to a Friend, 1633 (?)," in Orgel and Goldberg, *John Milton,* pp. 1–2.

7. John Milton, "Sonnet 7," in Orgel and Goldberg, *John Milton,* pp. 34–35.

8. Ibid.

9. John Milton, "Paradise Lost," Book IX, Lines 25–26, in Orgel and Goldberg, *John Milton,* p. 524.

For those of you who have yet to fasten upon a specific direction for your lives, I cite the example of Milton to remind you that you too have an "inward ripeness," for this is exactly what your Yale education has given you. What you have obtained with four years of effort is precious and important. You have sat with some of the best teachers in America, and their curiosity and their passion for learning have inspired you. You have learned to reason critically, to hold up ideas, beliefs, and experiences to rigorous scrutiny, to think for yourselves. You have the tools to shape your own lives, to set your course, and to meet life's challenges with energy and enthusiasm.

I trust that you have learned even more than this. Yale has taught you that a full life involves more than self-satisfaction; it requires as well a commitment to service—to family, community, and the larger society. Your deep involvement in the extracurricular life of the campus and the New Haven community gives me confidence that you have learned this lesson well.

Those of you who have a clear sense of direction may at certain moments wonder: "Is this it? Is my commitment to medicine, or law, or painting, or teaching something that will never be altered?" And, for those of you who have yet to choose, the fear of lost freedom may inhibit decisive action. By comparing Wordsworth and Milton, I do not mean to imply that the choice of a life plan is made once and for all. Indeed, to bring the matter closer to home, we might look at some of the astonishing mid-career transitions made by Yale College graduates.

Consider just these few examples. A lawyer, Class of 1961, builds a distinguished practice in the area of securities law, then becomes chief executive officer of a major manufacturing corporation. An entrepreneurial retailer, Class of 1950, builds a successful business, sells it, and then creates and produces one of the most successful musical comedies of all time. A member of the Class of 1984 wins two Academy Awards as an actress, then becomes one of Hollywood's leading directors. Finally, another entrepreneur, Class of 1963, develops a pioneering travel business, sells it, devotes the next decade to independent scholarship, and produces a strikingly original work documenting how our First Amendment freedoms were threatened in the early years of the Republic.

Women and men of the Class of 1997, early and late bloomers alike: it is time to graduate, to take the next step. Whether your course is now clear or still uncertain, you have prepared yourselves well during our four years together. Whether you are marked with outward confidence or "inward ripeness," you have encountered here great ideas, inspiring teachers, and extraordinary classmates. Make good use of the gifts that Yale has given you. Fill your lives with continued learning and devoted service. Recalling Milton's description of Adam and Eve leaving their first home: the world is all before you, where to choose your place of rest, and Providence your guide.

The Task of Citizenship

Four years ago, at your Freshman Assembly, I spoke to you about the task of self-discovery. I suggested that here at Yale you would encounter ideas and take them seriously, develop the capacity to think critically and independently, discover deep interests and consuming passions, and define the kind of person you want to be. This morning, I want to consider how the self interacts with the wider society. I want to reflect on the task of citizenship, on how you will use what you have learned at Yale to shape our nation and the world.

A little more than one hundred years ago, the historian Frederick Jackson Turner set forth a provocative thesis about the effect of the American environment on the character of the individual. I begin by quoting at some length:

> To the frontier the American intellect owes its striking characteristics. That coarseness and strength combined with acuteness and inquisitiveness; that practical, inventive turn of mind, quick to find expedients; that masterful grasp of material things, lacking in the artistic but powerful to effect great ends; that restless, nervous energy; that dominant individualism, working for good and for evil, and withal that buoyancy and exuberance which comes

Baccalaureate Address, May 24, 1998

with freedom—these are traits of the frontier, or traits called out elsewhere because of the existence of the frontier.[1]

It has been exactly a century since America's last territorial expansion, but the distinctive elements of American character described by Turner persist: independence, self-reliance, ingenuity, entrepreneurship. They manifest themselves today in the realms of scientific discovery, artistic creativity, and economic innovation—spheres of activity in which America leads the world. Even without new land to tame and cultivate, Americans continue to seek out new frontiers in every direction.

Turner believed that the distinctive traits of the American character had been shaped by the frontier, but their persistence in the absence of free land suggests that we must look beyond geography to explain them. Might not the persistence of independence and self-reliance also derive from America's openness to immigrants who came to its shores seeking freedom from religious persecution or economic deprivation? Might not the persistence of ingenuity and entrepreneurship also derive from the relative permeability of barriers to social and economic mobility in America? And does not the persistence of representative government and the individual rights embedded in our Constitution protect us from the kind of tyranny that might arbitrarily penalize the independent, self-reliant, ingenious, and entrepreneurial?

This line of thinking in fact predates Turner by a half century. In his classic study *Democracy in America,* Alexis de Tocqueville describes the American character in terms much like Turner's, but he sees the source of these traits in America's openness to immigrants, absence of hereditary class structure, and democratic institutions.

I am well aware that some scholars see America's history as a se-

1. Frederick Jackson Turner, "The Significance of the Frontier in American History," *Report of the American Historical Association, 1893,* reprinted in Turner, *The Frontier in American History* (Huntington, N.Y.: Robert E. Kreiger, 1976), p. 37.

quence of conflicts in which the interests of class (the ruling one), race (the white one), and gender (the male one) have prevailed again and again. But one need not join this debate to assert a mere fact: relative to other nations, the opportunities for social mobility and intellectual freedom in America have been and remain abundant. These opportunities have been seized by generations of citizens from a multitude of ethnic backgrounds. They have been, for the past several decades, increasingly available to women as well as men, to racial minorities as well as white Europeans.

Your university reflects this distinctive American openness, and you and your classmates are the assembled proof. You already give evidence of possessing those distinctive American traits. As individuals you have been shaped by American society and microcosms within it—family and university. These environments have given you abundant opportunities. As you graduate, it is now your responsibility to contribute to the shaping of the larger society and to preserve for others the opportunities that it has made available to you.

What does this responsibility entail? It requires, first of all, that you cherish the democratic institutions that support individual liberty. This means taking seriously your obligation as citizens. It is easy, too easy, to become cynical about involvement in public affairs, but, I assure you, if you and your contemporaries across the nation fail to participate in public life, and fail to serve when opportunities arise, you will undermine the very basis for your own freedom.

Your responsibility also entails participation in civic activities beyond those associated with politics or public life. Long ago, Tocqueville noted that the vitality of American democracy depended crucially on the exceptional degree to which its citizens joined together in voluntary associations directed toward civic betterment. As he observed:

> Americans of all ages, all conditions, and all dispositions constantly form associations. They have not only commercial and manufacturing companies, in which they all

take part, but associations of a thousand other kinds, religious, moral, serious, futile, general or restricted, enormous or diminutive. The Americans make associations to give entertainments, to found seminaries, to build inns, to construct churches, to diffuse books, to send missionaries to the antipodes; in this manner they found hospitals, prisons, and schools. . . . Nothing . . . is more deserving of our attention than the intellectual and moral associations of America.[2]

In recent years an apparent decline in civic participation through voluntary service has been noted and lamented. In a well-known article published three years ago, Robert Putnam reported some disturbing evidence.[3] Between 1973 and 1993, the number of Americans who attended, within the year prior to being surveyed, a public meeting on town or school affairs declined from 22 to 13 percent. Participation in parent-teacher organizations, the League of Women Voters, Boy Scouts, and the Red Cross also dropped dramatically. Overall, the Census Department's Current Population Survey indicates that between 1974 and 1989 there was a 16 percent decline in the number of adults who volunteered regularly in any civic organization.

The good news is that graduates of Yale College are not among those who have chosen to disregard their civic responsibilities. Recently, the Mellon Foundation conducted a survey of three cohorts of alumni that measured, among other things, their involvement in voluntary community service activities.[4] The three Yale College

2. Alexis de Tocqueville, *Democracy in America,* vol. 2 (New York: Vintage, 1945), pp. 114, 118.
3. The data that follow are reported in Robert D. Putnam, "Bowling Alone: America's Declining Social Capital," *Journal of Democracy,* January 1995, pp. 65–78.
4. I am grateful to William G. Bowen for granting me early access to the *College and Beyond* database recently assembled by the Mellon Foundation. Doug Mills provided timely and reliable computer assistance.

classes surveyed were two, fifteen, and forty years beyond graduation. Nearly two-thirds of the most recent graduates participated voluntarily in local civic activities and organizations, and 20 percent had leadership roles in such activities. Of the group fifteen years beyond graduation, more than two-thirds had served as volunteers since graduation, and nearly 30 percent had served as leaders. Of those forty years beyond graduation, 83 percent had participated as volunteers, and 56 percent had taken leadership positions.

If, to these local commitments, we add involvement with national charitable organizations and with environmental and conservation groups, the percentages of those who had participated in at least one volunteer activity rise even further. Among recent graduates, the participation rate was 71 percent, and 22 percent had leadership roles. Among the most senior of the alumni cohorts, the participation rate was 88 percent, and 60 percent had served in leadership positions.

I believe that you, the Class of 1998, will carry on this tradition of civic involvement, because of your outstanding record here at Yale. Hundreds of you have been actively engaged in community service. You have given music lessons at the Cooperative High School, taught chess to schoolchildren at the New Haven Free Public Library, read four times a week to third-graders at the Timothy Dwight School, written, directed, and produced plays performed by children from around the city, counseled teenage women at Troup Middle School, and organized a science fair for students at the Troup and Roberto Clemente schools. In these activities, and scores of others, you have helped others to develop the skills and self-confidence to take advantage of the opportunities that this country offers them.

Last week I received a letter from a second grade teacher in New Haven. She wrote:

> I have been teaching more than 28 years in New Haven and have NEVER had anyone stay as a volunteer in my classroom for two consecutive years, let alone four consecutive years!

[This] consistency while working with the children is particularly important to my students who often have much inconsistency in their lives . . .

They and I have been truly fortunate to have had [this] presence in the classroom weekly for the last four years.

This is just one example of what sustained involvement in a community can mean.

Women and men of the Class of 1998: You have been challenged by great teachers, confronted by new ideas, and stimulated by interaction with extraordinary classmates. You have had the opportunity to develop your powers of critical thinking and expression, and you have had the time to discover your own interests and passions. Each of you has acquired the capacity to learn and grow, and some of you, like Yale graduates in every class that has preceded you, will reach the very frontiers of human achievement.

Now it is time to use what you have learned here not only for personal fulfillment, but also for the benefit of the wider society. You are fortunate to live in a nation that gives opportunity to those with great potential; it is your responsibility to preserve that opportunity for others. Your generosity of spirit has made a difference for life on campus and in New Haven. May your generosity now expand to encompass America and the world.

Beyond Community Service
The Nation and the Wider World

F our years ago, at your Freshman Assembly, when you felt for the first time the great Newberry Organ rumble beneath your feet, when you saw officers, masters, and deans arrayed before you, I told you that you had come to a serious place. I told you that this is a place where ideas are taken seriously, where athletics, extracurricular activities, and community service are taken seriously, where involvement and moral responsibility are taken seriously.

In my attempt to predict what would be in store for you here, I suggested that you would come to appreciate the life of the mind, develop your capacity to think critically and independently, engage actively in something you feel passionately about, form friendships that you would treasure, and come to understand yourself more deeply than before. I also predicted that many of you would develop an interest in helping those around you.

Your record of involvement in our local New Haven community impressively confirms this last prediction. You have worked with schoolchildren, teenage mothers, battered women, the homeless, and those with mental retardation. Each semester, about half of you found time to engage on a regular basis in one or more of the many outreach programs affiliated with Dwight Hall, the Office of New Haven Affairs, the Athletics Department, or one of our professional schools or museums. In these activities you have come to understand

Baccalaureate Address, May 23, 1999

that the helper and the helped share a common humanity. Along with the knowledge and habits of mind you have acquired here, your experience in giving service has prepared you well for participation in and leadership of civic, religious, and community organizations.

What you have done for this city you must now do for your country and the wider world. I want to encourage you this morning to redirect at least some of your admirable energy for social betterment and service. I want to urge you to take more interest in public issues at the national and global level.

I recognize that on this score you might require some persuasion. Many of you have expressed to me disillusionment with the institutions of representative government and cynicism about the people who shape and conduct public policy. I think I understand some of the reasons for your disillusionment. Our nation often seems obsessed with the personal lives of its leaders and indifferent to their politics. Many politicians appear to be more concerned with tomorrow's newspapers than with the long-term consequences of their actions. We can't muster the will to enact meaningful gun control despite a murder rate vastly in excess of that in other developed nations. And we have recently entered a war without formulating clear strategic objectives and, seemingly, without thinking through many of the simplest and most probable contingencies.

It is all too easy to blame politicians, special-interest groups, television, or the press for the diminished quality of public discourse and the apparent incoherence of public policy. We must instead acknowledge that these are *our* problems. I remind you of what our nation's founders had to say about this, in *The Federalist,* no. 1, page 1: "It seems to have been reserved to the people of this country, by their conduct and example, to decide the important question, whether societies . . . are really capable or not of establishing good government from reflection and choice, or whether they are forever destined to depend . . . on accident and force." I recalled these powerful words of Alexander Hamilton two weeks ago as I listened to Jared Diamond, the noted scientist and winner of the Pulitzer Prize, who was on campus to deliver a lecture at the groundbreaking for our new environmental science facility. Diamond told the story of Easter Island, where the inhabitants built a flourishing culture best known for the enormous stone statues erected on the coast. The stone was quarried many miles from the sea and transported on the trunks of giant palm trees that served as wheels. The palm trees were subsequently used as levers to lift the stones into place, and then the trunks were carved into large sea-faring canoes, which ventured far from the island to harvest tuna and dolphin, the principal source of protein in the diet of the Easter Islanders. When the last palm tree was cut down, the natives turned for subsistence to the meager wildlife resources on the island, and ultimately to cannibalism. When European explorers arrived, the island was an uninhabited, barren wasteland.

How do such things happen? They happen for the same reason that avoidable wars and genocides have occurred repeatedly in this century. They happen because people go about their daily lives, seeking fulfillment for themselves and their families, without recognizing that large-scale forces are going awry and without taking action to reverse them. Hamilton's question is still open: it is up to us to determine whether our future is to be decided by "reflection and choice" or whether it is destined to depend on "accident and force."

Your generation of Americans has enjoyed material prosperity, the absence of general mobilization for war, and, although this work is still incomplete, unprecedented opportunity for members of minority populations. I want to suggest that these three blessings, which have established for you an environment in which you can choose freely the lives you wish to lead, haven't been conferred on you entirely by accident. Wise leadership and sound public policy have made a large contribution to shaping the conditions that allow you so much hope and promise.

Consider, for example, the benign state of our national economy. We prosper in large measure because we have a system that allows decentralized agents—individuals and firms—to seek profit in relatively free markets by responding to the abundant opportunities created by the rapid advance of scientific and technological knowledge. But the quality of public policy and national leadership has a powerful impact on how well the system works. For example, a long history of generous public funding for basic scientific research has contributed mightily to establishing the foundation of our current prosperity. More recently, the able leadership of Treasury Secretary Robert Rubin, a graduate of Yale Law School, and Federal Reserve Board Chair Alan Greenspan has prevented regional financial instability from causing a global depression.

Nor is it entirely an accident that we have avoided war on a substantial scale for the past quarter century. The collapse of Soviet Communism may have been inevitable, but our response to the collapse might easily have been mismanaged. During the crucial transition years we were fortunate to have an experienced foreign policy team in the White House. As their recent memoir illustrates, President George Bush, Yale College Class of 1948, and Brent Scowcroft, his National Security Adviser, wisely focused on the long-term global and strategic implications of the collapse of the Soviet Union and the reunification of Germany, rather than seeking short-term political advantage from these events.

Nor is it an accident that members of minority populations have greater opportunities in your generation than ever before. Here we all benefit from the concerted action of private citizens like Martin Luther King, Jr., and the millions of every color who voiced support for his position, as well as the political courage of President Lyndon Johnson, who pushed through legislation that has made an enduring difference.

I cite these examples to remind you that good government, and the action of citizens to encourage good government, has mattered, fundamentally, in your own lives. This is an important reminder because the issues I have just discussed—prosperity, peace, and racial justice—still demand our urgent attention. Because of improvements in health care and changes in family size since the Second World War, your prosperity in mid-life will depend profoundly on whether we seize the opportunity, now, to reform the Social Security System. The military action now under way in the Balkans makes it abundantly clear that we must design and maintain a consistent framework for global security that at once reduces the risk of nuclear confrontation and deters aggression and genocide. We must also recognize that, without substantial improvement in early childhood, elementary, and secondary education, too many children will be unprepared to take advantage of the career opportunities that are now potentially available to all citizens without regard to race or other circumstances of birth.

Finally, we must attend to the degradation of our global environment, lest we ourselves suffer the fate of Easter Islanders. If we fail to intervene, by the time your children graduate from college, nearly all of the world's rain forests will be gone. And by the time your great-grandchildren graduate, global temperatures will have risen between one and seven degrees centigrade. If we reach the high end of that range, the results would be catastrophic.

In all these matters—Social Security, international security, racial justice, and environmental protection—powerful interest groups will make it difficult to find and implement solutions. Still, your responsibility is clear. Your education here has prepared you to be thoughtful, reflective, intelligent citizens. The nation needs your involvement, and the wider world demands your attention. Public service and engaged citizenship are part of your Yale legacy. From twelve representatives in the Continental Congress to three of the last five presidents of the United States, many Yale graduates have distinguished themselves as public servants, while others, as private citizens, have strengthened our democracy by speaking, writing, or simply participating in the public arena. I urge you to perpetuate this legacy.

Women and men of the Class of 1999: To you much has been given, and from you much is expected. You have been given four years to develop good habits of mind, to pursue your passions, to appreciate your teachers, to cherish your classmates, to understand yourself more deeply. You have seized all these opportunities and more, and you are prepared to lead lives of great personal fulfillment and service to others. You have also been given the blessings of prosperity, peace, and justice, and the perpetuation of these blessings requires more than serving well your families and local communities. Get involved with public issues; participate in public life. Give the right answer to Hamilton's question. By your conduct and example liberate our democracy from dependence on accident and force. Your task is to shape the future by reflection and choice.

Reflections on Revolution

We are living in the midst of a revolution. Should you doubt it, just consider how rapidly the world has changed since you came to Yale four years ago. In September 1996 you couldn't buy groceries or health care products or airline tickets on the Internet. Amazon.com had been operating for a year, but HomeGrocer.com, drugstore.com, ShopLink.com, Priceline.com, and cheaptickets.com were not yet in business. Silicon Valley was booming, but Silicon Alley didn't exist. The Dow Jones Industrial Average was one half its current value, the NASDAQ index was one third its current value, and you couldn't check the weather forecast on the "wireless Web" using your cell phone.

You occupy a privileged position in this revolution, because, as Dean Brodhead just reminded you: "The world is all before you where to choose your place of rest." And Milton was not the only poet to describe the possibilities opened by revolution. In 1791, less than a year after leaving Cambridge, William Wordsworth headed off to Paris, where he was quickly caught up in the exhilaration of the early years of the French Revolution. He wrote: "Bliss was it in that dawn to be alive/But to be young was very heaven."[1] Wordsworth's

Baccalaureate Address, May 21, 2000

1. William Wordsworth, *The Prelude* (Text of 1805), edited by Ernest De Selincourt (London: Oxford University Press, revised impression, 1960), Book X, Lines 693–694.

revolution, as we know, descended into Terror and hence to Empire, but it changed the political and social structure of Europe forever.

The year I entered college, Bob Dylan wrote an anthem for my generation—"The Times They Are A-Changin'"—in which he described another revolution. What came to pass was less apocalyptic than he envisioned, but to the extent that he prophesized a revolution of attitude, he was on to something. In the wake of the turbulent 1960s, most Americans emerged with a profoundly revised perception of the rights of racial minorities and women, a belief that opportunity should not be constrained by race or gender. The enduring importance of these changes in attitude and objective opportunity should not be underestimated. But the 1960s did not radically alter the economic and social order.

By contrast, the Internet revolution will alter economy and society no less profoundly than the advent of the railroads in the nineteenth century and the automobile in the twentieth. The Internet will shrink time and space in much the same way—changing patterns of production and distribution, reorganizing the structure of business enterprises, rearranging people across the landscape, altering the relationship between home and work. The railroads gave a powerful impetus to productivity gains and economic growth by stimulating regional specialization in agriculture, the creation of the multidivisional enterprise, and the emergence of new, inland cities and financial centers like Atlanta and Dallas at important junctions. The railroads also spurred social change by distributing population linearly across the nation and radially from the center of larger cities.

The advent of automobiles, trucks, and highways had an equally profound effect on productivity and economic growth—allowing the decentralization of production and distribution, providing greater flexibility in location and scheduling, reducing barriers to entry, encouraging product differentiation and responsiveness to consumers. To the extent that suburbanization changed the life style of millions, transformed the use of leisure time, altered social structure, created disparity in educational opportunity, and threatened the viability of many cities, it would not be implausible to argue that the automobile was the most powerful agent of social change in the twentieth century.

If this evidence from economic history does not convince you, consider what Marcel Proust had to say about the coming of the automobile:

> Distances are only the relation of space to time and vary with it. We express the difficulty that we have in getting to a place in a system of miles or kilometers which becomes false as soon as that difficulty decreases. Art is modified by it also, since a village which seemed to be in a different world from some other village becomes its neighbor in a landscape whose dimensions are altered. In any case, to learn that there may perhaps exist a universe in which two and two make five and a straight line is not the shortest distance between two points would have astonished Albertine far less than to hear the driver say that it was easy to go in a single afternoon to Saint-Jean and Raspelière.[2]

The Internet will make ever more remote villages neighbors in a landscape whose dimensions are radically altered. Alongside this powerful tendency and its implied challenge to the cultural distinctiveness of nations and regions, the Internet promises gains in productivity that are commensurate with those attributed to the railroad and the automobile. We are only beginning to see how the Internet will revolutionize the marketing and distribution of goods and services. It will have similar effects on transactions done inside businesses and noncommercial organizations, even within the home. Everything we do that involves the acquisition and use of information is potentially subject to enormous cost saving, reorganization, and transformation. Exactly where all this will lead cannot be foretold,

2. Marcel Proust, *Remembrance of Things Past,* translated by C. K. Scott Moncrieff and Terence Kilmartin (New York: Vintage, 1982), volume 2, p. 1028.

but it is inevitable that tens of thousands of new business opportunities will arise and many old ways of doing business will become obsolete. For many transactions, national boundaries will become irrelevant. For many occupations, the physical link between home and workplace, relaxed by the automobile, will be obliterated. There will be big winners and many losers, and the net gains will be measured in rates of economic growth, at home and abroad, that substantially exceed those we have experienced for most of the second half of the twentieth century. This conclusion is likely to hold even if it turns out that financial markets currently overestimate the value of these developments.

All this implies a time of extraordinary opportunity for your generation. And you don't have to start a dot-com to participate. The possibilities for innovation and entrepreneurship extend well beyond the sphere of commercial activity into the nonprofit and public arenas. New forms of education will emerge, as well as new approaches to delivering social services and new instruments of public oversight and regulation

With these abundant opportunities to shape your own lives go important responsibilities. The benefits of these new technologies will not be shared equally by everyone. We will want to keep in place the powerful incentives that reward innovation, but we will not want to live with the consequences of an ever-widening gap between the rich and poor, in this country and around the world. The inchoate demonstrations in Seattle and Washington, D.C., as well as the re-emergence of political activism on this and other campuses, surely signal that there are important problems of social justice to be addressed, although the problems are not yet well formulated and the solutions not yet identified. As you seize the opportunities created by new technology you must also assume the burden of citizenship and share in the responsibility to spread those opportunities to others, who are now deprived of them by accident of birth or geography.

You are well prepared for the challenges of these revolutionary times, because, faithful to the values enunciated in the seminal Yale

Report of 1828, your education focused more on the "discipline of the mind" than on its "furniture." Your teachers were not mere "content providers." They helped you to develop the capacity to think independently, to master new bodies of knowledge as you confront them, to probe beneath the surface to seek the principles that organize the facts.

In this respect the education that you received here was instrumental. The capacity to think critically will serve you well as you build careers of every kind, whether in e-commerce, science, education, health care, social service, religion, or public life. And the experience here of living in community—of learning to work with and care for others—will serve you just as well as you face the moral and ethical challenges that attend a period of rapid social and economic change.

I ask you to consider just one more task. In the heady rush to seize the opportunities that this revolutionary time provides, and as you wrestle with the ethical dilemmas it presents, I would urge you to give sufficient time to reading and reflection. Your lives will be incalculably richer if you continue to challenge yourselves by reading and rereading the greatest works of literature, history, and philosophy. The humanities can be a constant source of enlargement for your lives.

I was inspired to this last observation very recently by reading the latest work of Yale's great scholar, critic, and teacher Harold Bloom. This slender volume, entitled *How to Read and Why,* is about the pleasures one derives from careful reading, and it makes its case by means of a series of examples drawn from short stories, poems, plays, and novels. Professor Bloom focuses on works of the imagination, on literature, but I would argue that serious engagement with great works of history, biography, and autobiography achieves the same result. Each of these forms permits the reader to encounter otherness—the independent consciousness of the poet, the fully developed characters of the great novelist or biographer, the richly drawn world of another time and place in which history unfolds. To give just one example, if we wished to understand the struggle between personal ideals and the necessity of practical action, we would be well advised to study both Tolstoy's portrayal of Pierre Bezuhov and the life and writings of Abraham Lincoln. By seriously engaging with the text, literary or historical, we both encounter difference, which through reflection enlarges our own sphere of experience, and we find a common humanity. These are my own words, but I believe they capture what Professor Bloom means when he draws upon Dr. Johnson, Francis Bacon, and Emerson to urge: "Find what comes truly near to you, that can be used for weighing and for considering. Read deeply . . . to share in that one nature that writes and reads."[3]

Reading, according to Bloom, will not make one behave better, nor will it change the world. One need not read with either objective in mind, because deep reading will enlarge your humanity, and this alone is worthwhile. But I would add this: reading, reflection, and action based upon reflection can make you a better person, and you can change the world.

Women and men of the Class of 2000: You are "standing on the top of golden hours."[4] Use what Yale has given you to make the most of these revolutionary times. Take care that the possibilities created by the Internet revolution are available to all. And keep on reading— to encounter otherness, to reflect upon it, to discover what binds you to those who wrote, to enlarge your humanity.

3. Harold Bloom, *How to Read and Why* (New York: Scribner, 2000), p. 29.
4. Wordsworth, *Prelude*, Book VI, Line 353.

China on My Mind

You are the three hundredth class to graduate from Yale College, or so it will say in tomorrow's Commencement program. Some of the more mathematically inclined among you might wonder: How could this be so? If Yale College is three hundred years old this year, and it takes four years to graduate, why isn't this the 297th commencement?

The surprising answer to this question is that some of our first students didn't require four years to graduate. Although the Collegiate School chartered in October 1701 held no commencement in the spring of 1702, there were two graduation ceremonies during the 1702–3 academic year. One of the first two students to be admitted came to the new college so well prepared that he was given both the B.A. and M.A. degrees in September 1702, while one of the six others who entered in the fall of 1702 graduated in the spring of 1703. Thus by the end of our second academic year we had already held two commencements, and we have had one each year ever since.

We have chosen to mark this tercentennial year not only with on-campus celebrations in October and April, but with events in Europe and Asia as well. Having progressed from local to regional to national institution during our first three centuries, we wanted to signal our intention to become a global university in our fourth. It is no coincidence that during the course of this year we announced the ex-

Baccalaureate Address, May 20, 2001

pansion of financial aid for international applicants to Yale College, the creation of new interdisciplinary professorships of international studies, the establishment of a new Center for the Study of Globalization, and the launching of the Yale World Fellows Program for emerging leaders.

Seeking to spread the word, I spent your examination period on a two-week visit to China, accompanied by a delegation of university officers, faculty members, and representatives of the Yale-China Association. In Hong Kong we celebrated the tercentennial with a symposium attended by nearly 500 alumni, parents, and friends from all over Asia. Then we met government officials and visited leading universities and schools in Beijing, Changsha, Ningbo, and Shanghai.

Yale's history of involvement with China is longer and deeper than that of any other university. Yung Wing, a member of the Yale College Class of 1854, was the first Chinese to receive an American degree. Remarkably, he was one of only ten international students in the entire university; today we have 1,500, including more than 300 from China. When Yung Wing returned home he became a strong advocate for the modernization of China, and he persuaded the emperor to establish an educational mission that sent more than one hundred Chinese boys to preparatory schools in the Connecticut Valley and then to colleges throughout New England. More than twenty came to Yale College, most notably Zhan Tianyou, who became a national hero for his role in building China's railroad system.

Later in the nineteenth century Yale became the first American university to teach the Chinese language, and at the time of our bicentennial a group of graduates launched what became the Yale-China Association. Yale-in-China, as it was originally called, established the Yali Middle School and the Hsiang-Ya Hospital, Medical School, and Nursing School. Over the years, legions of our graduates have had the opportunity to learn from the Chinese while serving as English teachers and health care workers at these and other locations. They invariably return with a deep appreciation and respect for the achievements of a culture that spans not just three centuries but six millennia.

Despite the long history of Yale's involvement with China, we were surprised by the enthusiastic response to our tercentennial visit. Our first day in Beijing was the lead story on the television news throughout China and front-page news in every newspaper. Such attention is not ordinarily showered on university presidents visiting the United States.

Perhaps the media attention had some connection with recent political developments, but I believe that the warm response that we encountered all over China signaled something deeper and more profound: how much and how intensely others aspire to share in the best of what we have in America.

This aspiration is one aspect of the many-faceted phenomenon we call globalization. The instantaneous transmission of ideas and images is bringing the world closer together. Cross-cultural influences have always been with us, but today they are more powerful because of their immediacy. This much is clear: the opening up of China that began in 1979, abetted by the advent of CNN and the Internet, marks a distinctive new chapter in the long and complicated relationship between China and the West. This relationship has been brilliantly traced by Yale's distinguished scholar of Chinese history, Jonathan Spence, whose lectures have been enjoyed by many of you, as well as by many of us here on the stage.

I know that some of you have serious concerns about certain aspects of globalization. In some parts of the world the fear of absorption by a common global culture has precipitated a strong reaction to protect local values and ethnic identities. I know far too little about China to predict where and in what form reaction to globalization will occur, but surely a 6,000-year-old culture will not yield easily to a mindless homogeneity, nor should it. Still, we learned from our own experience that the Chinese are embracing certain Western ideas and values. High school and university students alike are eager to learn more about our universities and how they might gain access to them, and faculty and administrators at China's leading universities are determined to reshape their institutions in the image of ours.

Our trip also reinforced for me the important lesson that there is a powerful complementarity between academic learning and direct experience. As an economist, I had read about Shanghai's astoundingly rapid growth, but, on the one hand, seeing the impressive new buildings rising in the Pudong district added something to my understanding that I could not have absorbed through reading. And, on the other hand, knowing something about economic development and urban planning enhanced the value of direct experience.

Here's a very simple example. Where others might have seen only beautiful skyscrapers, I could see how their beauty was enhanced by their being intelligently set apart from one another, with green spaces and smaller-scale buildings in between. This is what I mean by the complementarity of academic learning and direct experience. You will learn something if you go to China, but the more you know, the more you will learn.

For an American steeped in the Western tradition, China is at once exhilarating and disturbing. As the market economy grows, the government is creating a legal framework to support and regulate it. But the emerging rule of law, which is still a work in progress, has not been extended to protect freedom of expression or the rights of the accused to the degree expected in a Western democracy. The press remains tightly censored, and there have been numerous recent reports of arbitrary arrests and prolonged detentions.

Whether economic liberalization will lead to greater personal freedom and expanded human rights remains to be seen. Western governments will continue to press for this, but history suggests that Chinese leaders will not quickly agree to constraints on their own span of political and social control. Professor Spence's brilliant new narrative, *Treason by the Book,* serves to remind us of the exceptional efficiency with which the emperor tracked down and arrested dissenters nearly three centuries ago. Still, students and administrators at the universities we visited reported that they experienced little inhibition in speaking their minds, and business leaders expressed confidence that political liberalization would follow economic development, as it did in Taiwan, with a significant lag. One would have to conclude this: on the future of human rights in China, the jury is still out.

I am well aware that you may find these reflections remote from the pressing concerns of the moment, such as finding a job and a place to live. Down the road, however, you will need to think about the wider world. It is an inevitable consequence of globalization that the careers you build and the friendships you form will not be confined to our shores. In business, law, medicine, education, or social services, you are far more likely than your parents to spend part of your life abroad and to have worldwide networks of professional associates. In this context, China matters, because one-fifth of the world's population lives there. It matters whether freedom or repression prevails there.

Many Americans are not well equipped for the task of world citizenship. The mayor of Shanghai asked me why it is that every schoolchild in China can identify the author and date of our Declaration of Independence and so few of ours can identify when the Qing Dynasty fell, when the Long March occurred, and when the Communists took power. The mayor makes a telling point. I suspect that even some of you, unless you are among those devoted to Professor Spence, might fail the mayor's test.

Pass or fail, it is our hope and expectation that your Yale education has prepared you well for the challenge of understanding the world we inhabit. It is ultimately not the facts you know but what you make of them that matters. What you need, and what we have tried to encourage in you, is the capacity to think critically and independently, to master new bodies of knowledge as you confront them, and to fashion the principles that organize the facts. From reading your publications, meeting with you over lunch in your colleges, and participating in town meetings, I have plenty of evidence that you've learned to think for yourselves.

As you move on, I advise you to make use of this discipline to deepen your understanding of the wider world. Many of you have already made a substantial commitment to this task. Nearly 10 percent of you participated in Junior Year Abroad programs, and 13 percent of you have benefited or will benefit next year from fellowships for research and study abroad. But I would encourage all of you to travel, read, and reflect. Live abroad for a time if you can. The increasing interdependence of nations makes it all the more important to understand one another's values and perspective. Try to understand and respect cultural differences even as you shape and seek to live by your own principles.

Women and men of the tercentennial Class of 2001: As your university commits itself to more intensive study and deeper understanding of the world beyond our shores, commit yourselves to becoming informed global citizens. Remember that you share a common humanity with 6 billion people. If you embrace that perspective as you build your careers, raise your families, and serve your communities, your own humanity will be enlarged. Cherish your freedom, share with others the bounty of prosperity, and earn the blessing of peace.

Thinking About September 11

We hoped and expected that our spectacular tercentennial celebration last October would be the most memorable public event of your senior year. But by the time it occurred it had already been overshadowed by the events of September 11. The terrifying images of that morning will never leave us, but neither will the reaffirming image of our candlelight vigil that evening. Confronting shock, horror, and terrible uncertainty, we came together to affirm toleration in the face of hatred, humanity in the face of barbarism, civilization in the face of anarchy.

Not quite nine months later, uncertainty remains, but toleration, humanity, and civilization endure. We admire the bravery of the public servants and private citizens who helped others to safety on September 11. We admire the courage of the passengers who overcame their captors on Flight 93 over Pennsylvania. And we admire the devotion of the soldiers who have risked their lives in the war against terror. I think it entirely appropriate that as this year ends, we recall how it began, by remembering those who, wittingly or unwittingly, gave their lives in the cause of the freedom we enjoy. I would ask you to join me in a moment of silence.

How do we comprehend the meaning of September 11, for the nation, for the world, for our own lives? No doubt we will all wrestle

Baccalaureate Address, May 26, 2002

with these questions for some time to come, for September 11 revealed that we have much to learn—about the Islamic world, radical and moderate, about how America is perceived by others, about the conditions that give rise to extreme hatred and violence.

My own strategy in seeking to understand something difficult and elusive is to read—to read some things new but also many things familiar. To acquaint us with the new, we have been fortunate to have the intelligent commentary of Tom Friedman writing twice weekly in the *New York Times*,[1] the Sunday-night lecture series organized by John Gaddis and Cynthia Farrar, and the volume of thoughtful essays edited by Strobe Talbott and Nayan Chanda of our new Center for the Study of Globalization.[2] But we need also to draw on our own personal bibliographies for solace, insight, and inspiration.

The way in which we gather together disparate texts is beautifully captured in the metaphor of a fan suggested by the Russian poet Osip Mandelstam.[3] Imagine that each fold of one's own fan represents a favorite work of literature, science, history, or philosophy. When we collapse the fan, we bring together works that are widely separated in time and space. We thus create a unity that is neither temporal nor geographical, but integral to our own individual construction of reality. No doubt each of you has such a fan, composed of texts that give meaning and definition to the reality you construct.

As I reflect on September 11, I gather in certain folds of my own personal fan, some proximate, others very distant in time and space. Close together are some of my American icons—Jefferson, Adams, and Whitman. But they juxtapose with a man of the Old World, who in his time saw the New World more clearly and compre-

---

1. Now collected in Thomas L. Friedman, *Longitudes & Attitudes: Exploring the World After September 11* (New York: Farrar Straus Giroux, 2002).
2. Strobe Talbott and Nayan Chanda, eds., *The Age of Terror* (New York: Basic Books, 2001).
3. Mandelstam's metaphor is cited and developed by Wai Chee Dimock, "Literature for the Planet, *PMLA* 116, no. 1 (January 2001): 173–188. I thank Jane Levin for directing me to Professor Dimock's essay.

hensively than any of its inhabitants—Alexis de Tocqueville. He in turn is linked across time and space with a Latvian Jew who re-created himself as a British philosopher and historian of ideas—Isaiah Berlin. Berlin's ideas connect to the work of my faculty colleague María Rosa Menocal, to Sigmund Freud, and then finally to the Talmud. Each of these folds in my personal fan, each of these chapters in my intellectual history, has helped me to understand something about September 11 and the world we inhabit in its aftermath.

In Jefferson and Adams one finds a powerful sense of America's destiny, and by this I mean more than their prescient observation that the young nation would come to span the continent. Both also believed that the American example of commitment to personal freedom and democratic government would spread around the globe. In Jefferson's view, the extension of personal liberty and democratic institutions, along with the progress of science and scholarship, would foster continual improvement in the material and intellectual condition of humanity. And this progress was not to be deterred. In 1821, Jefferson wrote to Adams: "Even should the cloud of barbarism and despotism again obscure the science and liberties of Europe, this country remains to preserve and restore light and liberty to them. In short, the flames kindled on the 4th of July 1776 have spread over too much of the globe to be extinguished by the feeble engines of despotism."[4]

Walt Whitman, writing a half-century later, held the same vision of American leadership, even in the wake of a devastating civil war. By virtue of the rights asserted and protected by our founding documents and broadened by civil war, and by virtue of the development of a transcontinental railway and the invention of labor-saving machinery, Whitman believed that America had already established the political and material foundations for the unfettered realization of

4. Thomas Jefferson to John Adams, September 12, 1821, in *The Adams-Jefferson Letters: The Complete Correspondence Between Thomas Jefferson and Abigail and John Adams,* edited by Lester J. Cappon (Chapel Hill: University of North Carolina Press, 1959), p. 575.

human potential. In the next stage of America's development, Whitman expected a full flowering of the human capacity for self-expression in a literary, artistic, and philosophical renaissance that would radiate from the New World to the Old. "America," he wrote, "filling the present with greatest deeds and problems, . . . counts . . . for her justification and success . . . almost entirely on the future. Nor is that hope unwarranted. Today, ahead, though dimly yet, we see, in vistas, a copious, sane, gigantic offspring. For our New World I consider far less important for what it has done, or what it is, than for results to come."[5]

Despite the strong counterweight of isolationism, the idea that it is America's destiny to spread liberty and enlightenment throughout the world has had a powerful influence on American attitudes and behavior in the family of nations. Did not many of us recognize this Jeffersonian sentiment within ourselves in the aftermath of September 11: that it was our responsibility not simply to defend ourselves but to ensure that the entire world was safe from the disruptive forces of terrorism, safe for freedom and democratic self-determination? Indeed, might not the actions of the terrorists themselves be understood as a desperate response by those who perceived not only America's economic and military power, but also its materialism, its secularism, its popular culture, and its insistence on individual freedom and democracy as threatening a way of life based on deeply held and profoundly conservative religious beliefs?

In his brilliant and still unrivaled analysis of America and its fate in the world, the French visitor Tocqueville recognized in the 1830s that the triumph of liberty was not inevitable, nor was the American version of democracy necessarily suitable for universal export. We should heed Tocqueville, for in my experience no one else comes close to matching his 165-year record as a long-term forecaster. He correctly foresaw the elimination of hereditary rank and class distinc-

5. Walt Whitman, "Democratic Vistas," in *The Portable Walt Whitman*, edited by Mark Van Doren (New York: Viking Penguin, 1974), p. 317.

tions around the world. He explained why Russia and the United States would at a certain point become the world's dominant powers. And he noted that once distinctions of rank and social class had become attenuated, despotism was all the more to be feared because tyrants (think of Hitler and Stalin) would be capable of stripping their subjects of all vestiges of humanity in a manner previously unthinkable.

And so what is Tocqueville's lesson for us, in the wake of September 11? It is that if personal freedoms and democratic institutions are to flourish around the world, their form must adapt to local conditions—to the geography, history, culture, and traditions of other nations. If we are to champion the virtues of liberty and enlightenment around the globe, we will be more likely to succeed by recognizing and respecting cultural differences.

This brings me to another fold in my personal fan—to Isaiah Berlin, who, in contrast to Jefferson's faith in perfectibility, took as a favored quotation this line from Immanuel Kant: "Out of the crooked timber of humanity nothing straight was ever built." Berlin argues, contrary to Marx, that ideas have a powerful impact on history, and that such ideas often involve the pursuit of some ideal future state of being—a religious vision of paradise or a secular utopia such as Plato's republic, Marx's communism, or Hitler's *Reich*. Inevitably, such visions of an ideal world come into conflict with an intractable reality, visions become dogmas, and visionaries become tyrants. The Taliban and Al Qaeda provide us with examples of contemporary visions of perfectibility that have turned to hatred and violence. We must be wary that our American enthusiasm for institutions like our own does not lead us to mistreat those who do not embrace them.

Berlin gives us little solace other than to call for moderation; he urges us to take no single objective or doctrine as absolute, to balance competing claims, to live with ambiguity and make trade-offs. But in her brilliant new book, *The Ornament of the World,* Yale professor María Menocal gives us hope by showing us the remarkable example of fruitful coexistence among Muslims, Christians, and Jews for seven centuries in medieval Spain. The period was not entirely peaceful and was less than tolerant by modern standards, and for much of it either Muslims or Christians were politically dominant. Still, Professor Menocal describes a time and place in which separate scientific, philosophical, literary, and artistic cultures flourished both independently and interdependently. And, of course, medieval Spain is not the sole example of a society hospitable to widely diverse ethnic and religious groups. Though we are far from perfect, just look around this hall.

Let me come back to where I started. We have much to learn about the forces that have turned many against us, and we must shed our insularity and seek to comprehend them. We need not abandon our Jeffersonian passion for extending freedom and democracy around the globe, but we should temper our enthusiasm by the recognition that not all peoples are alike, that differences should be respected, that we aren't always right, and that we have sometimes acted badly. It makes sense to recognize that some cultures do not share our conception of human rights and democratic processes, and we should tailor our expectations accordingly. But even toleration has its limits. It makes no sense to tolerate those who violently threaten our life and liberty.

Freud once defined the goal of psychoanalysis in this way: "Where id was, there ego shall be."[6] This is also the task of statecraft. In confronting the terrible violence of September 11, in confronting the irrational hatred of our nation that is all too manifest in some parts of the world, stern discipline has been and sometimes will be necessary. But we will ultimately prevail only through reasoned engagement. We must work to alleviate the objective conditions— poverty, malnutrition, and disease—that give rise to hatred. But we must also counter with fact and reason the hatred that is rooted in irrational fantasy, acknowledge differences that cannot be reconciled, and find a peaceful way to live with them.

6. Sigmund Freud, "New Introductory Lectures to Psychoanalysis," in *Standard Edition of the Complete Psychological Works of Sigmund Freud,* edited by James Strachey (London: Hogarth, 1966), volume 22, p. 80.

This is all very serious business, but, to keep it in perspective, we must remember that September 11 did not change everything. As you leave here you are entering a world in the midst of revolutionary transformations wrought by science and technology. We have in our grasp the capacity to alleviate poverty and malnutrition, to protect the planet from further degradation of its environment, to prolong human life and improve its quality. We have and will continue to develop the technology to accomplish these hitherto unimaginable goals; we need only the will. You have the opportunity to shape lives that produce both private happiness and public good. I know that you will rise to this challenge.

Women and men of the Yale College Class of 2002: I congratulate you on your extraordinary accomplishment and wish you success in every endeavor.

As you reflect on the world you are entering, after graduation, after September 11, I leave you with one more fold of my personal fan, the one I have tried to live by, from the section of the Talmud known as the *Pirke Avot,* the aphorism of Rabbi Tarphon: "You are not required to complete the work, but neither are you free to desist from it."

We cannot build a perfect world, but we must strive, you must strive—in your families and communities, in this nation and around the globe—to build a better one.

Building a Better Yale

Yale's Fourth Century

As Yale approaches the three hundredth anniversary of its founding, it is instructive to reflect on how the university has developed over the course of the past century. Physically, the campus has changed almost beyond recognition. Connecticut Hall, completed in 1753, and eight nineteenth-century structures on the Old Campus are the only academic buildings that survive from Yale's first two centuries. Other structures built as private residences in the eighteenth and nineteenth centuries have come into the university's possession during the past hundred years, but 90 percent of our square footage was built in this century—most of it between the world wars and much of it thanks to the extraordinary generosity of the Sterling and Harkness families. We strain to imagine such a radical physical transformation of Yale in the next century.

The academic enterprise has also changed substantially. We have added three new schools—Forestry, Nursing, and Management—merged the Sheffield Scientific School into Yale College and the Graduate School, and spawned three descendants of the School of Fine Arts—Art, Architecture, and Drama. The Graduate School, established in 1892, has matured into one of the world's great centers for the education of scholars and scientists. The School of Medicine has evolved from a modest training ground for physicians to a major enterprise of biomedical research and clinical practice that generates

Published October 1996 to stimulate discussion of Yale's future more than 40 percent of the university's revenues and expenses. In the Faculty of Arts and Sciences, many new departments and programs have been established. Some have thrived and earned great distinction—for example, Molecular Biophysics and Biochemistry, and American Studies. Other initiatives have been abandoned or supplanted—for example, the Departments of Education and Industrial Administration.

Amid all this change in our academic programs, the college described in Owen Johnson's 1911 novel, *Stover at Yale,* has not entirely vanished. Our undergraduates still value energy, affiliation, and achievement. Athletics, journalism, and political debate still thrive. But with the introduction of the residential colleges in the 1930s, the elimination of racial and religious barriers to admission in the early 1960s, the admission of women in 1969, and the more or less steady increase in the number of applicants over the past five decades, Yale College has become more open, democratic, and meritocratic.

In the many publications celebrating Yale's bicentennial there is virtually no evidence that the physical and demographic transformation of Yale, or the growth of science and graduate education, were foreseen at the turn of this century. As we enter the next century, we should not presume that we have greater clairvoyance than our predecessors. Some possibilities for improvement are discernible on the horizon, but many remain invisible. This report highlights some changes we can now foresee and describes principles that will guide our response to opportunities yet unseen.

We reach this point in Yale's history against a backdrop of national skepticism about the management and direction of our universities. In newspapers and news magazines, on talk shows, in the halls of Congress, even in some of our most prestigious journals of opinion, we see a number of complaints repeated frequently: the cost of a college education is too high; professors spend too little time teaching; universities should be doing more for the communities that surround them. There is also a pervasive sense, not entirely unjustified, that universities have been slow to adopt productivity-enhancing methods of management that might allow them to deliver their services more efficiently and more responsively. Even within the Yale community, students, parents, and alumni question our ability to control costs, the effectiveness with which the university is managed, and the long-term viability of our commitments to costly institutions, such as need-blind admissions and the tenure system.

This skepticism has infected public policy. Despite extraordinary achievements in expanding the frontiers of scientific knowledge, and despite the powerful linkages from new scientific knowledge to industrial technology and national economic competitiveness, the federal government seems disinclined to support the continued growth of university-based research, and the principle, adopted as public policy a half-century ago, that universities should recover the full cost of research supported by federal grants and contracts has already been significantly eroded. Despite remarkable expansion of access to institutions of higher education, federal aid to students has failed to keep pace with the cost of education. In 1979, Yale College awarded $6.9 million in need-based grant aid, of which the federal government paid $1.7 million, or 25 percent. By 1996, the amount of need-based aid granted to undergraduates had grown to $28.5 million, of which the government supplied $2 million, only 7 percent of the total.

Although Yale is not immune to these broad social forces impinging on the nation's universities, our abundant human and material resources justify optimism as we enter our fourth century. But to maintain and enhance the greatness of this university, we must have clarity about our mission. We must understand our distinctive strengths, for all great universities are not alike, and all should not respond alike to the challenges of the future. In this report I call for a reaffirmation of two important values that distinguish Yale from comparable institutions, identify two areas of distinctive strength, and offer two principles to help us make intelligent decisions as we chart the university's course in the years ahead.

Yale's Mission and Distinctiveness

As I observed in my Inaugural Address, Yale is a monument to human achievement. We preserve that achievement in our collections of books and manuscripts, works of art and architecture, objects and artifacts. We foster a capacity to appreciate that achievement by our teaching, and we augment it by our research.

Yale is one of the very few universities in the world with the tangible assets, human resources, and internal culture to make possible simultaneous dedication to the preservation, transmission, and advancement of knowledge. Most of America's three thousand colleges and universities are devoted primarily to teaching. Perhaps no more than one hundred are also major centers of research, and perhaps no more than a dozen of these have the libraries and collections to qualify as major centers for the preservation of our natural and cultural heritage. Yet even within this small group of universities with a common mission are characteristics that further distinguish Yale.

Two such characteristics warrant reaffirmation as we develop a strategy for our fourth century. First, among the nation's finest research universities, Yale is distinctively committed to excellence in undergraduate education. Second, in our graduate and professional schools as well as in Yale College, we are committed to the education of leaders.

These values are not merely rhetorical; each requires corollary commitments to policies, programs, and the investment of resources. Let me explore some of these implications.

Undergraduate Education

As at other institutions that aspire to leadership in the generation of new knowledge, faculty in the humanities, social, and natural sciences at Yale are hired and promoted with the expectation that they will make important and internationally recognized contributions in research. But Yale is distinctive in its insistence that members of the Faculty of Arts and Sciences teach undergraduates regularly. We expect undergraduate teaching to be taken seriously, and the example set by respected scholars who excel at teaching creates an environment in which good teaching is valued. The excellence and seriousness of Yale undergraduates rewards the faculty's effort and reinforces its commitment. There is an institutional cost to this; we cannot attract scholars who wish to escape teaching. But the benefit far outweighs the cost. Surveys of recent graduates indicate a very high degree of satisfaction with the education that Yale College provides.

At the center of the undergraduate experience is a liberal education, which develops a student's capacity to think critically and independently, laying the foundation for a lifetime of learning. But an outstanding undergraduate program must do more than cultivate the intellect; it must provide opportunities for the development of character. Our students participate in an exceptionally rich array of extracurricular activities: athletics, music, drama, publications, political organizations, and community service. To sustain the vitality of these activities we must invest in athletic facilities and equipment, space and resources for undergraduate organizations, transportation and other assistance for students engaged in community service. We must also provide excellent advising, counseling, and career services for our students.

The residential college system is one of Yale's most distinctive assets. Each college is an intimate community of about four hundred students—a liberal arts college within a research university. Because each residential college mirrors the entire undergraduate population, including students of all backgrounds and interests, Yale has been well protected from the social fragmentation seen on many other campuses. Each college offers seminars, hosts speakers, organizes social events, sponsors intramural teams, and provides counseling and tutoring. To make certain that the colleges remain strong centers of campus social and intellectual life, we will invest more than $200 million over the next decade to renovate thoroughly these extraordinary facilities, creating within them additional space for student activities, improving the quality and flexibility of our dining programs, and increasing the frequency of routine maintenance once major capital improvements are in place.

For Yale College to remain attractive to the best undergraduates, we must also invest substantially in the new information technologies that allow our students previously unimagined access to information and ease of communication. We have accelerated the pace of developing a high-speed campus computer network; every student room is now wired for high-speed computing, and shortly we will have broadband video capability in every room as well. We are initiating new programs to encourage the faculty to develop and adopt creative new applications of information technology in the classroom. We must embrace new technology with enthusiasm, encourage experimentation, and seize opportunities to provide remote teaching services, as well as access to our library and museum resources, to students and scholars around the country. We have already made some remarkable advances in the provision of medical services over the network, and we see an enormous potential for our faculty to have educational impact beyond New Haven. At the same time, we must preserve in Yale College abundant opportunity for small group, face-to-face discussion.

Educating Leaders

Academic excellence must remain the most important single criterion for admission to Yale's programs of study, but in our graduate and professional schools, as well as in Yale College, we should continue to look for something more—for those elusive qualities of character that give young men and women the potential to have an impact on the world, to make contributions to the larger society through their scholarly, artistic, and professional achievements, and to work and to encourage others to work for the betterment of the human condition.

To educate leaders for the twenty-first century we must renew some institutional commitments and initiate others. To give priority to the development of leadership skills we must sustain our investments in support of extracurricular activities, student organizations, and athletics. We must continue to seek students who can provide leadership to all segments of our heterogeneous American society. And we must continue to provide, to all who qualify for admission to Yale College, sufficient financial aid to guarantee that the cost of a Yale education does not prevent the matriculation of those with the greatest potential for excellence and leadership.

Beyond these commitments, we must recognize that the leaders of the twenty-first century, in virtually every calling and profession, will operate in a global environment. To prepare our students for leadership, our curriculum needs to focus increasingly on international concerns; our student populations must have strong international representation, and our students should have ample opportunities for study abroad. We have already made great strides in the internationalization of our curriculum. The content of many social science, law, and business courses is far more international today than it was even two decades ago, and enrollment in foreign-language courses is at an all-time high. We have many international students in our graduate programs, and we have recently begun to admit a significant number of international students to Yale College. We intend to continue on that course and also to expand the opportunities for Yale College students to study abroad.

Though our perspective must be global, we must not lose sight of the abundant opportunities for leadership here in the city of New Haven. More than two thousand Yale students, as well as many of our faculty, are actively engaged in volunteer service on a regular basis. This involvement pervades each of our professional schools—from Medicine and Nursing to Management and Divinity—as well as Yale College and the Graduate School. We must nurture this manifest sense of civic responsibility in our students, and, as New Haven's largest corporate citizen, we must assume leadership as an institution in community efforts to improve education and health care, revitalize neighborhoods, and foster economic development.

In emphasizing characteristics that distinguish Yale from other leading research universities—our focus on undergraduates and the education of leaders—let me not overlook the important tasks which we undertake in common with all leading research universities. Foremost among these are the advancement of human knowledge and the education of the next generation of scholars to carry on that mission. To support research, as well as to preserve our extraordinary collections, we have begun a $46 million program to renovate Sterling Memorial Library and to relocate our superb Music Library collections to a new facility within Sterling. We have built two major new science buildings within the past seven years, and we are planning to renovate or replace most of the remaining laboratory space. Our graduate students receive superior instruction in the development of their capacities for scholarship, but we must expand and improve the programs that prepare them to be teachers. We must also provide better advice, counseling, and assistance in finding positions both inside and outside the academy. The new McDougal Center in the Hall of Graduate Studies will begin to address these needs.

Yale's Academic Strengths

To be counted among the world's great universities, a certain degree of breadth is required. To retain our position in this select company, we must continue to prepare students for scholarship and practice across a wide range of disciplines and professions, and we must continue to advance knowledge across an equally broad spectrum. In all these activities—in every division of the arts and sciences and in every professional school—we aspire to excellence, and in most of them we stand among the world's leaders. No university, however, has the resources to be the best in the world in every area of study. We must strive for excellence in everything we do, but we cannot do everything.

In the preceding sections I have discussed certain values that distinguish Yale and described some of the investments we must make to uphold them in the future. But Yale's distinctiveness derives not only from its institutional values but also from its particular academic strengths. In a university in which excellence is pervasive, two constellations of activity exhibit unusual breadth and depth. Before moving to a discussion of principles that can help guide decisions as we enter our fourth century, I think it useful to characterize in broad terms these fields of study in which Yale has, and has the potential to sustain, special excellence.

The first of these is the humanities and the arts, broadly construed to include not only the humanities departments of the Faculty of Arts and Sciences, but also the fine arts schools, and our library and museum collections. I would include the Law School under this heading, given its distinctive emphasis on grounding the study of law in its philosophical and social foundations.

Yale is arguably the premier university in the world in the humanities and the arts. Four humanities departments (English, French, Comparative Literature, and History) were rated first in the most recent National Research Council rankings of the quality of faculty. In art, drama, and music, Yale's professional schools compete primarily with specialized schools and conservatories rather than other university-based schools, and yet the Schools of Art and Drama stand at the very top of their peer groups, and the Schools of Music and Architecture rank among the leaders. The Law School's preeminence is widely recognized, and only one other school in the nation can rival the breadth and depth of our library and art collections.

Yale's excellence in these subjects is not unconnected with its strength as an undergraduate institution. Exposure to some of the world's leading scholars in the humanities, to the richness of our collections, and, for the very talented, to musicians and artists of distinction, makes Yale College especially stimulating. We should be mindful, however, that it has taken decades to establish Yale's eminence in this constellation of activities, and that maintaining our distinction will require effort and investment. We must continue to employ the highest standards in making faculty appointments, and we must be willing, in an era when many universities aspire to leadership, to make highly competitive offers to attract and retain the best, in these fields as in others. To retain our competitive advantages in attracting fine arts faculty and students we must provide more resources for financial aid. We must find ways to house our art collections that will make more of the objects accessible, and our library collections must be protected from deterioration. Over the past two years we have developed an ambitious plan to provide new or renovated facilities for the Schools of Art, Architecture, and Drama, the Department of the History of Art, the University Art Gallery, and a newly consolidated Arts Library.

Yale's second great constellation of academic strength resides in the biological sciences and medicine. We are among the handful of centers in the world that have assumed leadership in the basic biological sciences, the understanding of human health, the treatment of human disease, and the education of scientists and medical practitioners. We consistently rank among the nation's leaders in grants awarded by the National Institutes of Health, and our M.D. and Ph.D. programs stand among the best. As our fourth century begins, we must aspire to continuing leadership in the life sciences, which hold so much promise for human health and our nation's future prosperity.

Maintaining excellence in the sciences, physical and biological alike, will require substantial resources to support both ongoing operations and capital investments. We have recently developed a plan for the comprehensive renovation and reconfiguration of our central campus science facilities, and a similar plan will soon be developed in the School of Medicine. This planning effort has clarified the trade-offs among the competing objectives of maintaining the size and quality of the faculty, the size and quality of our graduate programs, and the quantity and quality of renovated space. To finance the needed investments, with the prospects for federal support uncertain, we must obtain increased support for both capital improvements and operating expenses from nongovernmental sources: individuals, corporations, and foundations, as well as income generated from the transfer of university-owned technology to commercial use.

Guiding Principles for the Future

As we contemplate the future, we need to develop principles to guide the allocation of resources across activities. Let me suggest two such principles.

First, Yale's programs should be shaped more by an aspiration to excellence than a compulsion to comprehensiveness. Second, we should recognize and take advantage of the substantial interconnectedness among our schools, departments, and programs.

These principles of selective excellence and interconnectedness have important substantive implications, which I will illustrate by means of a few examples.

Selective Excellence

The range of human knowledge is so vast and so rich in variation that not even a great university can aspire to comprehensive coverage of every subject worthy of study. Even within those areas of Yale's greatest strength, the increasing specialization of faculty and the proliferation of sub-fields make comprehensiveness unattainable.

The principle of selective excellence has special relevance in fields of study—such as the physical sciences, engineering, and management—where limits on our resources will constrain our scale. In these fields, as in some others, faculty tend to identify with research "groups" that are narrower than whole departments or schools. In such instances, rather than seek broad coverage of an entire discipline, it may be wise to build a few distinguished groups of faculty who can compete with the best in the world in their areas of specialization for research support and graduate students.

Several departments at Yale—such as Astronomy, Statistics, and, more recently, Linguistics—have employed this strategy with considerable success. They have built distinguished faculties who concentrated their research in just a few areas of specialization, and within these areas the departments have become international leaders. We are now employing such a strategy in our three engineering departments. We do not intend to grow to the size of MIT or Stanford in these disciplines, but we believe we can develop internationally recognized research groups in a few areas of chemical, electrical, and mechanical engineering and still offer an excellent and broad undergraduate program.

We intend to apply the principle of selective excellence within departments and programs rather than among them. Instead of focusing on which programs and departments to eliminate, we will focus on how particular programs and departments can achieve and sustain excellence with limited resources. We have many examples within the university; several of our most highly regarded departments and professional schools are not among the largest in their peer groups.

Interconnectedness

President Giamatti often emphasized Yale's distinctive interconnectedness. The College, the Graduate School, and the ten professional schools do not stand independently. They are instead part of one integrated whole, lending strength and support to one another. In such an environment, faculty appointments and programs that span more than one school or department can often yield extra benefits for the university as a whole. Allocating resources at the intersection of schools and departments can have a powerful impact on scholarship, teaching, and the larger society.

As an example, consider the contribution of our fine arts schools to the quality of education and student life at Yale College. Because none of our peer institutions can match our array of professional schools in the arts, the involvement of faculty from the Schools of Art and Music in undergraduate instruction gives Yale College a natural advantage in recruiting the students with exceptional artistic or musical talent who prefer a liberal education to a specialized conservatory. And despite the lack of formal involvement of the School of Drama in undergraduate education, the very presence of the nation's finest graduate program, and the environment it creates through the Yale Repertory Theatre and graduate student productions, strengthens both the Theater Studies major and extracurricular dramatic programs, helping Yale College attract and nurture extraordinarily talented undergraduates with an interest in the theater.

Several departments and schools within the university are currently emphasizing interconnectedness as a central feature of their faculty development strategies. The School of Forestry and Environmental Studies has recently made a joint appointment with the School of Law, and it is exploring linkages with Biology, Divinity, Epidemiology and Public Health, and Management. And our engineering departments are looking to develop the field of computer engineering, drawing on Yale's existing strengths in computer science and applied mathematics, as well as biomedical engineering.

Interdisciplinary programs are another obvious means of drawing on the resources of twelve separate schools. As we approach Yale's fourth century, two university-wide programs have special importance: international studies and environmental studies. The Yale Center for International and Area Studies, now housed in a splendid new facility, Luce Hall, has historically drawn most of its faculty and student participation from the humanities and social science departments. Today, the School of Medicine is developing important teaching and research programs abroad, and Law, Management, Forestry and Environmental Studies, and Epidemiology and Public Health are undertaking new international initiatives. The Center for International and Area Studies can help to encourage and facilitate such efforts, drawing together students and faculty from around the university.

Similarly, because environmental issues are certain to remain among the public's paramount concerns as we enter the twenty-first century, we expect the contribution of Yale's Institute for Biospheric Studies to assume increasing importance. Sponsoring interdisciplinary research and graduate programs in the environmental sciences, the institute has drawn upon faculty in biology, geology, anthropology, and the School of Forestry and Environmental Studies. Further linkages with the social sciences, law, public health, and medicine are being developed. Strengthening our undergraduate program in environmental studies is also a priority.

Entering Yale's Fourth Century

We enter Yale's fourth century with a firm foundation and a clear direction. We reaffirm those values that have made Yale distinctive among the world's great universities—a commitment to undergraduate education and a determination to educate leaders. We have unique excellence in the humanities and the arts, and we have the capacity to sustain it. We stand among the world's best in the biological sciences and medicine, and we are prepared to maintain our position despite near-term threats of diminished external support. We intend to sustain and enhance excellence in all our academic endeavors, selectively, as our resources permit. And to achieve that excellence, we will draw strength from the interconnectedness of this place, from a whole that is greater than the sum of its parts, a single university.

Like our predecessors a hundred years ago, we have highly imperfect foresight. We cannot say what Yale will be in fifty or one hundred years, but our strategy for the first decade or two is clear enough. To maintain Yale's distinctive strengths, we will invest, on a scale not seen since the 1930s, in the renewal of our residential colleges and libraries, as well as our athletic, arts, and science facilities. We will move aggressively to reap the fruits of the new information technologies in our teaching, research, and communication. We will build our competency in those areas of teaching and research that will assume increasing importance in the foreseeable future—such as international and environmental studies. Indeed, we will continue the transformation of Yale, begun in the eighteenth century, from a local to a regional to a national and now to a truly international institution—

international in the composition of its faculty and student body, as well as in the objects of its study.

We have thought hard about how to marshal the means to realize our aspirations, and I believe that we have the financial and organizational capacity to succeed. But we need also to be flexible and adaptive. We are engaged in the generation of new knowledge, and this core activity will inevitably produce new opportunities for as yet unimagined innovations in education and research. Thus, we can have no rigid long-term plan. Instead, there must be a broad consensus on values, a shared sense of direction, and a perpetual willingness to revise yesterday's plans on the basis of new knowledge. In this spirit, we enter Yale's fourth century with confidence and commitment.

Yale at 300

We gather here in front of the Sterling Library to commemorate a unique moment, the three hundredth anniversary of the founding of Yale University. A century ago, not one of these beautiful buildings framing the Cross Campus was yet in place. When our predecessors gathered in Battell Chapel to mark Yale's bicentennial, they had barely a glimmer of what the university might become. Although Yale was widely recognized as one of the nation's leading educational institutions, its population of students, faculty, and staff did not begin to mirror the nation and the world as it does today. No one anticipated that during the century to come the physical size of the university would increase by a factor of ten, the student body by a factor of four, the faculty by a factor of eight, library holdings by a factor of thirty, and the endowment, adjusted for inflation, by a factor of one hundred and twenty.

Try to imagine a Yale augmented by these multiples a century from now. Imagine a university with 110 million square feet, 44,000 students, 16,000 faculty, 300 million books, and an endowment of $1.3 trillion. Such numbers are unthinkable to us, as today's numbers would have been to our precursors. And they are certainly not inevitable. Our view of the road ahead is no better than the view in 1901. Who, then, when fewer than 100 courses were offered, would

Tercentennial Address, October 5, 2001

have imagined that Yale College students would have 2,000 courses to choose among a century later?

Like our predecessors, we cannot see into the distant future. But at such moments of commemoration we serve ourselves well by summing up where we are and where we are headed. I want to approach this task by discussing, in turn, five specific and very significant contributions that Yale, along with America's other great universities, makes to our society.

The first of these contributions is to educate citizens and leaders who think critically and independently. The second is to model freedom of expression and freedom of inquiry in a nation committed to freedom. The third is to serve as an engine of economic growth and prosperity for our society. The fourth, more recent in origin, is to foster the development of the community that surrounds us. The fifth, of increasing importance in the years ahead, is to promote greater understanding among the peoples and nations of the world.

The justly famous 1828 *Report of the Faculty of Yale College* provided a definition of liberal education that has stood the test of time: "By a liberal education has been understood, such a course of discipline in the arts and sciences, as is best calculated, . . . both to strengthen and enlarge the faculties of mind, and to familiarize it with the leading principles of the great objects of human investigation and knowledge." The faculty recognized then as now that what it called the "furniture" of the mind—the great objects of human investigation—should properly evolve over time. And during the past century, as the "furniture" changed, faculties at Yale and elsewhere have come to focus more sharply on the other attribute of a liberal education, the "discipline" of the mind.

Consider how pedagogy has evolved in the past century. As recently as the 1930s and '40s, "recitation" of the contents of a textbook or a lecture was the most widely practiced method of eliciting student participation in class. By the 1960s the participatory seminar and the discussion section afforded students the opportunity to present and defend their views. Today, in class as well as on written assignments and examinations, students are judged more on the quality of analysis and argument than on the ability to recall facts.

Our insistence on developing in our students the capacity for reason, reflection, and independent critical thinking produces graduates who are equipped with curiosity and the capacity to adapt to ever changing work and home environments, graduates with the flexibility and imagination to put new ideas into practice. Our pedagogy also produces citizens and leaders with a capacity to think clearly about public issues and to contribute meaningfully to the debate and discussion that is the life-blood of our democracy.

All this said, this is no time for complacency about the quality of education. It has been three decades since Yale College undertook a comprehensive review of its curriculum. At this moment the university is in the midst of making substantial investments to support research in science, engineering, health care, and environmental studies to complement its long-standing strength in the humanities and social sciences, and we are investing heavily in our fine arts schools, our museums, and our local community. Although we are justly proud of the quality of undergraduate education at Yale, we must not let this moment pass without considering how undergraduates might share in the benefits of these university-wide investments. I have asked Dean Brodhead to take the leadership of a major study of education in Yale College. Rather than confine this work to a small faculty committee working in isolation, this study will involve many faculty, students, and recent graduates, who will solicit ideas and suggestions from the entire Yale family. We expect the study to require most of this academic year and the next to produce a final report and recommendations.

The second contribution made by Yale among other leading universities is especially important at this moment of national crisis. It is, above all, our commitment to freedom that makes America still a beacon of hope for humanity. And our universities have a crucial role in the preservation of this essential value. In our commitment to freedom of expression and freedom of inquiry we have been, and we must remain in a world radically changed by the events of September 11, a model for the nation.

Our commitment to free expression and free inquiry is inextricably linked to the pedagogy that I have just described. Those educated to think critically are the most disinclined to fall under the sway of prejudice, to succumb to intolerance, to close their minds to debate and discussion. It is no accident that our universities have historically been bastions in defense of free inquiry, no accident that within Eastern Europe and China they have been oases of free expression.

America faces difficult choices in the months and years ahead: how to strike a balance between civil liberty and security at home, and a balance among diplomatic, economic, and military actions abroad. By drawing on the accumulated knowledge of our faculties, our universities have much of substance to contribute to this discussion. To be most effective, we must be willing to tolerate dissent from a national consensus, but we must also resist convergence toward a consensus of dissent. We must think creatively and rigorously about how to cope with new threats to world order and, at the same time, listen with tolerance and openness to all points of view. Our universities must remain places in which opinions on every side can be expressed and subjected to critical scrutiny. This is the great legacy of the Enlightenment that inspired both the founding documents of our nation and the intellectual tradition of its universities.

I turn now to the third important contribution that universities make to the larger society, an area in which Yale is committed to making its largest investments in the years ahead. During the past half century, America's economic strength has increasingly come to depend on its leadership in translating advances in scientific knowledge into new products, new services, and entire new industries. During this same period, as a result of conscious and far-sighted decisions taken during the Truman administration, America's universities have become the principal worldwide source of new scientific discovery. It is therefore no exaggeration to say that America's universities are the wellsprings of our prosperity.

The national system of science established after World War II has three essential features. First, the federal government bears the principal responsibility for funding basic scientific research. Second, universities—rather than government laboratories, nonteaching research institutes, or private industry—are the primary institutions in which this government-funded research is undertaken. And third, most federal funds are allocated not according to commercial or political considerations but through an intensely competitive process of review conducted by independent experts who judge proposals on their scientific merit alone. Within the overall constraints set by the federal budget, there is a virtual free market in ideas.

This is a uniquely American system, and it has been an overwhelming success. Over the past three decades, the United States has been the source of about 35 percent of all scientific publications worldwide, and more than 60 percent of the world's Nobel prizes have been awarded to Americans or foreign nationals working in American universities. Along with facilitating unimagined improvements in human health, university-based research has been ultimately responsible for the development of information technology, the Internet, biotechnology, and the modern pharmaceutical industry.

In the decade ahead we will invest nearly $1 billion in facilities to support research in science, engineering, and medicine. Our announcement of these ambitious plans two years ago has already helped us to recruit exceptional scientists and engineers from around the globe. No investment is more important to securing Yale's position among the world's leading universities, and no investment holds greater promise for the health and prosperity of the nation and the planet.

The science-based revolutions that have propelled the American economy have at the same time left behind millions affected by the flight of manufacturing industries, first from our cities, then from our shores. The plight of our inner cities—insufficient job opportunities, substandard housing, and underperforming public schools—threatens the health of the republic. Increasingly, our universities have been expected to shoulder some responsibility for the improvement of our cities.

Such an expectation is entirely appropriate. With the decline of urban manufacturing, universities are now the largest employment sector not only in New Haven and Cambridge, but also in Philadelphia, San Francisco, San Diego, Indianapolis, Birmingham, Alabama, and Provo, Utah. Institutions of higher education are well suited to the task of urban citizenship because faculty, students, staff, and alumni possess valuable skills and expertise, and universities have a stake in making their surrounding communities more attractive to prospective students and faculty. We also have a commitment, within our walls, to ensuring the full development of human potential. It is natural to extend, where we can, this possibility to our neighbors.

Eight years ago I committed the university to a substantial mobilization of voluntary effort and to investments in support of economic development, neighborhood revitalization, and public education. We have worked, as never before, with city government officials, business leaders, clergy, and neighborhood organizations. Signs of progress in our collaborations with New Haven surround us—from downtown to Broadway to the Dwight neighborhood, to increased home ownership throughout the city, a burgeoning biotechnology sector, and thriving partnerships with several public schools. The relationship between New Haven and Yale has become a model for the nation.

In the years ahead I hope that we can achieve the same kind of progress with our labor unions, whose members make an essential and valuable contribution to the life of the university. We are eager to work with Locals 34 and 35 to find a new way of structuring our relationship, relying on day-to-day collaboration rather than periodic confrontation. Just as our work with the city of New Haven required participants on both sides of the town-gown divide to cast aside long-held prejudices, working collaboratively with our unions will require participants on both sides to overcome years of distrust. This is not easy to accomplish, but our work in the city has demonstrated what is possible.

As most of you know, we have celebrated our tercentennial year not simply here at home but also in Europe, Asia, and Latin America to mark Yale's intention to become a truly global institution. This aspiration underscores another potentially significant contribution of our major universities to the wider society. Through the subjects and students we teach and the educational and research collaborations we undertake abroad, we can advance greater understanding among the world's peoples. We can also contribute to the solution of problems that cannot be contained within national borders—such as the spread of disease, the degradation of the environment, and, as we now know all too well, the rise of terrorism.

In step with our sister institutions in higher education, we have in recent decades greatly expanded the presence of international subject matter in our curriculum. We now teach fifty-two languages, offer more than six hundred courses on international topics, and sponsor research and teaching programs focused on each of the world's major regions. More than 30 percent of our Ph.D. students and 8 percent of our undergraduates are neither citizens nor permanent residents of the United States. We recently launched our Center for the Study of Globalization, a fellowship program for emerging international leaders, exchange programs with universities around the globe, and more than twenty educational and research partnerships with universities, health care organizations, and government agencies in China alone. To enhance our capacity to attract the most able students from around the world, in this tercentennial year we extended to international applicants to Yale College the benefits of need-blind admissions and full need-based financial aid—one of the great legacies of our third century.

Some of you may wonder why I have focused my remarks at least as much on the American research university in general as on Yale in particular. This emphasis is not accidental. One of the most powerful developments of Yale's third century has been the augmentation of the role that our universities play in the life of the nation. We strive to make Yale distinctive, and through the fortunate confluence of past history and present resolve we have succeeded in standing among the very best. Nonetheless, we are linked inextricably with our sister institutions in a common enterprise. And here is the task before us: to educate thinking citizens and leaders, to preserve free inquiry and free expression, to generate new knowledge that improves health and spreads prosperity, to encourage realization of the human potential latent within our cities, and to reach out to the world to provide a foundation for mutual understanding and peace. *Hoc virtutis opus.* This is the work of Yale's fourth century. When our successors gather here one hundred years from now, may they look with favor on what we have accomplished.

Honoring Schools, Teachers, and Traditions

An Embryonic Democracy

I am greatly honored to be here today to celebrate with you this important moment. Francis Parker School has a very special place not only in Chicago but in the nation, because it was and remains a noble experiment in progressive learning and an enduring monument to the ideas of John Dewey. It seems especially appropriate that I should be here on this occasion, and not simply because of my personal status as one married, as it were, into the Parker family. I also represent an educational institution with noble aspirations—one that has benefited enormously over the years from the presence of brilliant, curious, and creative graduates of Francis Parker. I can assure you that Parker's mark is at least as notable at that other school, the one that we in New Haven refer to as "the Latin of the Northeast."[1]

I was recently reminded of the importance of such consecrating moments by remarks given on a similar occasion by my colleague, Tony Kronman, the dean of the Yale Law School. Dean Kronman recalled these words of Cicero: "In no other realm does human excellence approach so closely the paths of the gods as it does in the founding of new and in the preservation of already founded communities."

The Romans were, of course, experts in the practice of founda-

Remarks on the dedication of a new building at the Francis Parker School, Chicago, on September 12, 1998
1. The Latin School in Chicago is Francis Parker's traditional rival.

tion and preservation. Wherever they built, the Romans marked the occasion with solemn ceremony, just as we do today. Those presiding over such dedications were known as "augurers," one of the four colleges of the Roman priesthood. It was the task of the augurers to consecrate the site of a new building and to interpret the omens that foretold the future of the enterprise to be housed therein. Foretelling is in fact the root meaning of the Latin verb *inaugurare,* from which we have derived the word inaugurate. The English word has by now lost its specific connection with the ancient practice of augury—foretelling and consecrating the future; today, the act of inauguration connotes merely marking, and perhaps blessing, a beginning. I, for one, am relieved to be liberated from this ancient burden. I am happy to be here to mark this new beginning for the Francis Parker School, and equally happy that you do not expect me to read tea leaves, cast lots, interpret signs, or otherwise magically foresee the future.

Dean Kronman reminds us, however, that the word *inaugurare* had another, older verbal root, *augere,* which means simply to increase or add to something already present. For the Romans, every new beginning, every inauguration, was also an augmentation of what had gone before, a rededication of something already under way, a resumption of earlier ambitions. So now we are on more comfortable ground. The future may be unknowable, but, if this marvelous augmentation of what already exists at the Francis Parker School stands in proper harmony with what has gone before, if it is faithful to the spirit of this place, if it provides the means of carrying on Parker's important mission—one already consecrated by nearly a century of cherished experience—then we can truly say that all augurs well for Parker's future.

So let me say a few words about the traditions to which Parker must rededicate itself today, and let me try to accomplish this by telling you how I first learned about the existence of the Francis Parker School.

The story begins in the fall of 1964, in a section of freshman English at Stanford University. Our first writing assignment was to describe, in an essay of three pages, a place of special significance. One day, during the second week of the term, our earnest and rather nervous instructor returned to us this first writing assignment, telling us that she would like to read aloud one particularly outstanding submission. As she began, I was, shall we say, surprised. In high school, whenever the teacher read a student's paper aloud, it had always been mine. I suppose you can guess whose paper was chosen this time.

Rummaging around in our attic a few weeks ago, I came upon a cardboard box filled with artifacts of this particular author's college years. On yellowing pages of "erasable" paper (Do you remember "erasable" paper, that relic of the typewriter age?), I found the essay she had written in our freshman English class. I quote:

> The first thirteen years of my education were bounded by the crumbling walls of an English Tudor home. The structure was actually built as a school, but it so closely resembled a home with a front hall and a wood-burning fireplace, curiously shaped rooms and secret hiding places, that its inhabitants always referred to it as such.
>
> The building was unique, to say the least. The queer, gabled roof was topped with a weathervane pointing perpetually east. On the front of the school was a clock, stuck, for some unknown reason, at twenty minutes past seven, and a mask of ivy scraggled over the walls. The attic was filled with memorabilia of a bygone era, including the skeleton of a student named Phoebe. Locked in the attic, she starved to death during one Christmas vacation. Once a year the fourth grade visited her, a martyr to disobedience, for students were forbidden to visit the attic alone.
>
> The narrow stairs leading down from the attic terminated in the German room, a tiny space under the eaves with the Rhine River sloping across its ceiling. The ceiling of the eighth grade room was strange also, because a boy

had once built a boat in the attic and a hole had to be cut in the floor to remove it. . . . Along the walls of the third floor hall, above the musty physics equipment, was a mural of the philosophic development of man, painted by a student in the early mornings before school started. Both the chemistry laboratory and the fourth grade room below had balconies. The balcony in the fourth grade was filled with trunks of Greek costumes, and many a Greek warrior charged down the stairs to attack the Trojans below. The cubbyhole under the stairs was a nice place, too, for reading or telling secrets.

Rereading this description of the old school confirms me in two judgments. The first is this: to have made such a vivid impression, Francis Parker must have been a very special place. And the second judgment is this: over the years, I have made no mistake in asking Jane to edit my writings.

Not mentioned in Jane's essay is the inscription in the auditorium. "A school should be a model home, a complete community, an embryonic democracy." By the way, anyone who has spent more than thirty years at family dinners with the three Aries girls knows that in this summary of the school's aspirations there are sixty-three letters. And though Jane's essay omits the motto, she attests to its truth. I quote again:

The character of the building was mirrored in its students. In looking at a class, one saw not a smooth surface, but a rich texture of individuals. Privacy in a world this small and complete was virtually impossible; but individuality was nurtured. . . . The school became for many people the reason for their existence. . . . School was conceived of as lasting not from 8:15 to 3:11, but from age four to eighteen. It was a way of life, not part of another life—a culture with its own traditions, customs, beliefs, and ideals. . . .

There were those to whom the conception of a life beyond the walls of 330 Webster Avenue seemed impossible. For us the tall black iron fence encircling the school marked the boundary of the world. Within was reality.

It is remarkable that as a college freshman, Jane understood how Parker was a model home and a complete community, even as it nurtured individuality. What she could not possibly understand in 1964 was how enduring a stamp Parker placed upon its graduates. Married as I am into a Parker family, I have come to know many graduates of the school, and I am unfailingly impressed by something I have found in all of them. Wherever their lives have taken them, whatever careers they have chosen, they read, they think about what they read, and they talk about what they read. They are engaged with ideas.

This should not be taken for granted. It is not every excellent private school that can make such a claim. Something about the Parker experience stimulates the love of learning. And this cannot be simply because Parker is a supportive environment, a model home, a complete community. For Jane's generation, I have no doubt, it was because Parker had an imaginative, challenging curriculum and extraordinary teachers. Lynn Martin's fourth grade focused entirely on Greek civilization; if there is a better way to encourage a passion for reading and learning, I haven't heard about it. And who cares if Barr McCutcheon refused to call sines, cosines, and integrals by their right names? He inspired hundreds and hundreds of students to appreciate the beauty of mathematics.

You have here, within these buildings old and new, a great legacy: a school with a history, a school with a soul. There are marvelous traditions to be carried forward: Morning Ex, County Fair, Class Day, Big Brothers and Sisters. But most important among these is devotion to the life of the mind, to the kindling of curiosity, to awakening within each child an appreciation of ideas. If these traditions are given life in this beautiful new addition, then past and future will be harmonized, and no augurer need apply.

A Salute to Princeton

The evidence is sketchy, but there is reason to believe that the event we celebrate today had its origins nearly eight hundred and thirty years ago. In 1167, according to the account of John of Salisbury, foreign scholars were expelled from France, sending back to their homeland the Englishmen who studied at the University of Paris. At the same time, to strengthen his hand against the influence of Thomas à Becket, Henry II prohibited English clerics from visiting the Continent without permission of the crown. In the wake of these two developments—the one bringing English scholars home and the other restraining their travel abroad—a growing concentration of scholars settled in and around Oxford, where a great university began to emerge in the waning years of the twelfth century.

Thus began the great academic procession. In the thirteenth century the influence of Oxford's newly established collegiate system spread to Cambridge, and, nearly four centuries later, Cambridge-educated citizens of the Massachusetts colony founded the school that soon became Harvard, importing from their alma mater a Trinity College dropout to serve as its first head. Sixty-five years later it was a graduate of Harvard, James Pierpont, who secured a charter for the new Collegiate School of Connecticut, which soon thereafter took the surname of its benefactor, Elihu Yale. After another forty-five

Delivered on the occasion of Princeton University's 250th Anniversary, Princeton, New Jersey, October 25, 1996 years, as President Rudenstine has explained, six blues and a fellow traveler founded the great university whose birthday we mark today. Paris, Oxford, Cambridge, Harvard, Yale, Princeton, and beyond, the procession continued as graduates of our three colonial institutions went on to found many if not most of the leading colleges and universities throughout North America.

President Rudenstine has reminded us of the fate of Princeton's first presidents. I would add to his account one notable lesson about the shortcomings of university governance that we all failed to learn from that early experience. It is true that Jonathan Edwards came to Princeton in poor health. For this very reason, when he arrived, the wise men of the College of New Jersey convened a group to determine whether the Reverend Edwards should be inoculated against smallpox. For days the group debated the question, dangling the Reverend Edwards over the fire like the spider of his best-known sermon. At last, after much scholarly deliberation the decision was taken to go forward with the inoculation. And so Jonathan Edwards, Yale's greatest theologian and preacher, died—killed by a Princeton committee!

We have long forgiven this transgression, even as we have forgotten the lesson it teaches about the dangers of decision-making by committee. Indeed, we have come to admire Princeton's agreeable atmosphere, its magnificent walks, its proud athletic tradition, and, above all, its distinguished graduates and superb faculty. For any university, to have educated Madison and Wilson and to have welcomed and nurtured Einstein and von Neumann would be accomplishment enough for a quarter millennium.

It is my great honor, on behalf of Yale University, to bring greetings and congratulations to Princeton University on the occasion of your 250th anniversary. In expressing our hopes for Princeton's future, we at Yale are drawn to these words of one of your most distinguished graduates, Adlai Stevenson:

> We [Americans] have placed our hopes on the understanding of our people. It is a magnificent gamble. And it

is to the universities, to Princeton, that we look for so very much. How well it does its job determines how each generation resolves that magnificent gamble, for it involves the idea of freedom and the search for truth.

We can have no higher hope or aspiration for Princeton but that it will do it well.

For myself and for my institution I can add only that we have no higher hope or aspiration for ourselves than to join with Princeton in this noble calling, to join with Princeton in the nation's service.

Remembering Oxford

I am honored, most deeply and profoundly honored, by the recognition conferred on me today. If I am deserving, it is only because the institution I represent has proved itself a worthy de-
scendent of this great and ancient university, the center of learning for
all English-speaking peoples for three-quarters of a millennium.

It is customary to identify the righteous Puritans who founded
Yale as great-grandchildren of Oxford. The lineage runs through one
Cambridge and then another. But the connection is also more direct.
Although Yale's founders at the dawn of the eighteenth century were
Harvard men, the idea of a college in New Haven was conceived and
pursued more than half a century earlier by an Oxford man, John
Davenport, the founder and spiritual leader of the New Haven
colony. A dissatisfied early overseer of Harvard, the learned theocrat
tried repeatedly to raise funds for a new college, but even the scan-
dalous deviation of Harvard's first president on the question of infant
baptism failed to spur the citizens of New Haven to open their purses.

Three centuries after John Davenport's last attempt to found a
college in New Haven, Jane and I reversed the journey of the Puritan
forefathers and found earthly paradise right here in Oxford. It was
1968, and the New World was in turmoil. As our friends at home
burned candles, draft cards, and buildings, we discovered within

Remarks on receiving an honorary doctorate at Oxford University, November 23,
1998

these high walls a kingdom of the mind. Following the advice of Sir Isaiah Berlin, I spent my first year here reading philosophy and then wrote a B.Litt. thesis on Max Weber which, thankfully, no one save my adviser and examiners has ever read. I continue to believe, nonetheless, that whatever clarity of mind and expression I possess is attributable to the discipline forced on me in my Oxford tutorials. One example will suffice to bring home the point. After months of having my essays on various subjects torn to shreds, I wrote a paper developing a variant of Karl Popper's argument that the future of scientific knowledge cannot be predicted. My tutor, a distinguished philosopher, offered but one comment: "Well done, but the argument is anthropocentric." Puzzled, I asked for further clarification. He replied: "What you say may be true for human beings, but it might not hold for intelligent beings on other planets." To this day, I don't know whether he was being perfectly serious or whether this was his way of telling me that I had at last made a convincing argument.

Oxford not only sharpened my thinking; it also made both Jane and me aware of the special pleasures of scholarship and teaching. The thorough and passionate engagement of our Oxford teachers with the real and imagined worlds of history and literature inspired us and filled us with admiration. It amazed us that Roger Highfield, my mentor at Merton, was so intimately acquainted with every detail of the history of our college that he might walk through a time warp to the fourteenth century and not for a moment feel himself a stranger. And it delighted us that Jane's tutor at Lady Margaret Hall, its beloved Vice Principal Katherine Lea, was herself on intimate terms with the literary figures who were her life's work and love. Once, after Jane's enthusiasm for Wordsworth became evident, Miss Lea confided in her: "You might read Dorothy Wordsworth's journals," she said. "I don't think she would mind."

For thirty years I have been grateful to have had a glimpse of this marvelous world that is Oxford University. Today, my gratitude overflows.

Chasing After Society

Ihave often found it useful to invoke the fragment from Archilochus brought to our attention by Isaiah Berlin in his famous essay on Tolstoy's view of history: "The fox knows many things, but the hedgehog knows one big thing." To remind you, Aristotle and Shakespeare were foxes, while Plato and Marx were hedgehogs. Bill Parker, like Tolstoy, was a fox who wanted to be a hedgehog.

For more than thirty years he kept refining the collection of boxes and arrows that he called the "great schema," a diagram intended to explain the movement of Western economic history. Over time the categories evolved from simple to complex, from materialistic to humanistic, from categories like "natural resources," "technology," and "capital stock" to categories like "greed," "power," and "self-expression." Bill knew that I was a sucker for these diagrams, having spent a year of my youth studying Max Weber, and he shared with me every permutation. But Bill was much too much a fox to really believe that the movement of history could be reduced to a single page, however intricately it depicted the connections and feedbacks among human motivations and physical constraints. In the end, in the last essay among his collected papers on Europe and the world economy, he produced a brilliant, self-revealing account of his quest for the "one big thing"—not quite admitting failure but much too self-aware to claim victory. What other economic

Eulogy for William N. Parker, Philip Golden Bartlett Professor Emeritus of Economic History at Yale, May 5, 2000 historian would dare confess that his real object in measuring productivity growth was to "reach the mysteries of the human heart"?

Bill's grasp of the particular, rather than his quest for the general, made him not only a great historian but a storyteller, a writer, a poet, and an astute observer of people. Alas, the subtlety of the fox is not so easily appreciated by economists as is the boldness of the hedgehog. When the Nobel prize committee finally got around to economic history, it opted for the hedgehogs. This is not to fault the selection of two of Bill's worthy colleagues, only to note that there are those of us who prefer *The Marriage of Figaro* to the final movement of the Ninth Symphony.

It is well known that Bill was the most productive of mentors. His students occupy chairs in economic history at Harvard, Stanford, Berkeley, and Northwestern. But his influence as a teacher and counselor extends far beyond economic history. In his thirteen years as director of graduate studies in economics he touched hundreds of lives, exuding warmth and extending kindness to every student while privately relishing their idiosyncrasies. He could give an empathetic capsule psycho-biography of every one of us. Despite, or was it because of, his own Middle Western rectitude he relished the rebels most of all; he had a special fondness for my entering Class of 1970, a notorious collection of radicals, most of whom didn't really like economics all that much.

I have always counted myself among Bill's students. I loved his course on European economic history, and my appreciation deepened when I served as his teaching assistant. The year after that Bill was on leave, but he pleaded with me to serve once again, never revealing his true purpose, which was this: he wanted to ensure that the visitor replacing him, his former student Jan deVries, would not deviate too far from the wisdom of the master.

Bill guided me through my early years of professional development, generously arranging invitations to meetings and conferences. Jane and I were entertained by Bill and Yvonne countless times; they always included us when the opportunity arose to meet a visitor of interest. Bill also provided advice on how to behave properly. I'll never forget our first faculty dinner party at the Parkers'. Vicki Parker babysat for us that evening, and when I went to pick her up Bill came to the door in his most elegant dark suit, white shirt, and tie. I was wearing corduroy pants and a turtleneck sweater under a sport jacket. As I left with Vicki, Bill said to me gently, "I suppose you will be going home to change." I got the message.

To close, I succumb to the irresistible temptation to quote the master himself. In the concluding passage of the aforementioned autobiographical essay, Bill captures not simply a vision of history, but also a vision of himself and his relationship to his students.

> Where will it all end? Writers of discourses such as this lack a sense of completion if they fail to end their books on a note of fashionable pessimism. After all, it is a lazy scholar's "out" to predict an end to history, since then one is under no obligation to go on with the chronicle. But professors who teach students see society in its most hopeful, reproductive phase. It is not uncommon for those, in their heart of hearts, to fantasize a vision of civilizations stretching as far ahead into the future as they have back into the past, and continuing like those past civilizations to reel erratically and convulsively down the corridors of Time. On such a moving panorama of civilizations, they often discern, too, figures of intellectuals, continuing to chase after their societies, a sheaf of rattling papers in hand, as one chases after a busy department chairman, trying to get in a word as he or she rushes off, late for a meeting.[1]

May we, the paper-rattling friends and colleagues of Bill Parker, continue to chase after society, all the while caring for our students and for each other as he cared for his students and for us.

1. William N. Parker, *Europe, America, and the Wider World* (Cambridge: Cambridge University Press, 1984), volume 1, p. 255.

James Tobin
Scholar-Hero

J im was all of a piece. As a teacher, departmental colleague, citizen of the university, economist, and shaper of public policy, his influence on us derived from two sources—his crystal-clear intelligence and his moral seriousness.

These two aspects of Jim's nature correspond exactly to the reasons he chose economics as a vocation in the late 1930s. In his own words, economic theory was a "fascinating intellectual challenge," and it had "obvious relevance to understanding and perhaps overcoming the great depression and all the frightening political developments associated with it throughout the world." As a teacher and colleague, Jim conveyed with every ounce of his being these two lessons: economics was rigorous and beautiful, and it mattered.

In my first year of graduate school Jim played only a cameo role in the theory course, entering to deliver a few lectures on each of two unrelated topics: externalities and the life-cycle model of consumption and savings. I can testify that there was nothing theatrical about Jim's classroom style. He was not a charismatic or dynamic lecturer. Still, I remember his classes on these two subjects as if he had given them yesterday. We were terrified novices in his presence, but he nonetheless began each class as Socrates, posing questions as if he expected us to have the answers. Miraculously, he turned every wander-

Eulogy for James Tobin, Nobel Laureate and Sterling Professor Emeritus of Economics at Yale, April 27, 2002

ing answer to true north as he moved from questioner to lecturer. He was so clear, so coherent, so perfect that one understood not only the particular models he explicated and their limitations, but also how one might ask and answer a large family of questions in the same conceptual neighborhood. It seems astonishing to say this, but in two classes on the life-cycle model I believe Jim gave us all we needed to understand every argument that has been offered in the past thirty years of debate on how to finance the Social Security system.

As colleague and sometime department chair, Jim set the tone for us all. His passion for both the beauty and relevance of economics inspired and motivated nearly all the junior faculty of my generation and those preceding it. Even for those of us working at some distance from Jim's principal areas of interest, he was our intellectual hero. Though none of us traveled so far, we all followed in his path.

Jim also taught us how to be citizens of the university. I was fortunate early in my career to serve on the committee that came to bear his name, charged in 1980 with reconsidering all aspects of the procedures and criteria for the appointment and promotion of faculty. For Jim, such a task demanded the same high level of intellectual rigor and moral seriousness as any work of scholarship. The Tobin report is more than a set of recommendations. It is a wise and learned treatise on how a great university develops its faculty, and how it should fairly balance such competing considerations as demonstrated scholarly achievement, future potential, teaching, and citizenship. The report is as clear, logical, and coherent as any Tobin lecture or article. For me, however, the enduring significance of the Tobin Committee was not the content of its report but the method of its work. If a question is worth asking, it is worth bringing to bear the full power of one's intellect and the full range of one's moral sensibility.

Jim was in a class by himself, possessing virtues rarely combined in the same person. He was a towering scholar and a moral hero. We will never forget him.

A Devoted Mentor

When I first came to graduate school at Yale in the fall of 1970, the entering students gathered in the Cowles basement to be welcomed by the chairman and the director of graduate studies. After the faculty left, some of the returning graduate students brought in pizza and beer. Then they proceeded to tell us what the Yale department of economics was really all about. I remember talking to Mike Krashinsky, then a second-year student. He strongly recommended that I depart from the standard first-year curriculum of micro, macro, history, and econometrics—and substitute for one of them a second-year elective course. Not just any course, but one, amid the drudgery of mastering the tools of the trade, that would remind me why I had decided to go to graduate school in the first place.

The course I chose was Economics 140: "Market Organization and Public Policy." This week I pulled out my file on the course. Looking at the syllabus, my notes, and an eight-page handout given to us at the first meeting of the class, I was astonished. The first thing to flash into my head was the memory of a passionate high school French teacher of European origin, known simply as "Madame," whose teaching style bore no resemblance whatsoever to Dick Nelson's. Whenever one of her students made a particularly egregious er-

Remarks delivered October 14, 2000, on the seventieth birthday of Richard R. Nelson, George Blumenthal Professor of International and Public Affairs, Columbia University, and a Yale professor from 1968 to 1986

200

ror of grammar or pronunciation, Madame would sputter with frustration: "*Vous vous faites ridicule.*" And then, in English, she would say: "You learned that on the first day of French."

I had always thought that Madame exaggerated, but I am no longer sure. Consider first the syllabus from Economics 140. It was marked up with extensive notes, taken on the first day. Of course, Dick had started off the class, as was his custom, by giving us a "road map." Now that I have read most of the items on the list, I can see that Dick's observations divide neatly into two groups. About three-quarters of my notes characterize succinctly and accurately the central point of the paper; the other notations are more idiosyncratic—not the first thing most people would say about the article in question, but something offbeat, subtle, provocative, and, in most if not all cases, right.

Consider also the eight-page handout given to us that first day. Now I am not saying that it contained the fully developed evolutionary theory of economic change. It just said something like this: to understand complex policy issues we must first understand institutional context, how market and nonmarket methods of control and regulation actually influence the behavior of organizations and individuals within them, and how the search for improvement—which from one perspective can be regarded as solving optimization problems within a given system—is ultimately transformative of that system. This last strand leads to both a theory of organizational change and a theory of technological change and market dynamics. In a word, I suppose we did learn everything on the first day of French.

We are here tonight because somewhere along the line we were each seduced by Dick Nelson, inspired by his striking originality and encouraged to open our eyes and look at the world differently. He taught us, and he made us wiser, broader, and better economists, social scientists, policy-makers, and leaders. And though we were attracted to Dick by the freshness and power of his ideas, our continuing admiration of him derives not only from his intellect but his character. Dick's curiosity and devotion to ideas is thoroughly matched by his warmth and devotion to friends, colleagues, and students. I, for one, have never known a better or more devoted mentor.

In the economics department at Yale, Dick made every one of his students and junior faculty colleagues feel welcome and appreciated. At the end of every semester there was always a party for the industrial organization students at Dick and Katherine's home on Blake Road. Only after I became a faculty member did I realize how painfully shy most of the students were at the beginning of these parties, and how Dick—circulating, smiling, and engaging everyone—worked at loosening them up. Dick's generous spirit reached out to all the junior faculty members in applied microeconomics, not just to former students like me. He always had time for conversation and was always willing to read drafts and find a way to praise them even as he offered penetrating criticism. Truly a full-service mentor, Dick even found a summer vacation house for us to rent on Cape Cod, right next door to his own. Jane and I cherish the memory of many beautiful evenings with Dick and Katherine on their deck overlooking Sheep Pond.

We salute Dick Nelson: thank you for giving us a road map, and thank you for so brilliantly and generously lighting the way.

Shimon Peres

When I was a boy growing up in San Francisco, my family belonged to Congregation Sherith Israel, which held services in a beautiful synagogue in the Romanesque style. During services—which often seemed to me to go on for a very long time—my brother and I did not always give the devoted attention we might have to the prayers or to the rabbi's teachings. Instead, I am afraid, we would stare up at the dome, which was encircled by a single row containing a great many light bulbs. We used to occupy ourselves by counting the lights. I can tell you even today that there were sixty-seven. Although yesterday I checked this number with my brother and he insists that there were sixty-six.

I would not blame you for thinking that by counting light bulbs I wasted my opportunity for religious education. But, alas, just above the ring of lights was written around the dome this one sentence from the prophet Micah (6:8): "It hath been told thee, O Man, what is good, and what the Lord doth require of thee: only to do justice, to love mercy, and to walk humbly with thy God."

I often think that had my religious education taught me nothing more than this, Dayenu, it would have been enough. These words of the prophet are at the heart of Judaism: they prescribe the ethical behavior that is the essence of a good life, a life in the service of the covenant.

Introductory remarks at the Chubb Lecture of Shimon Peres, then the Prime Minister of Israel, February 11, 1997

I know of no man in our era who embodies these words more than Shimon Peres. A keen sense of justice, deep and abiding compassion for all peoples, and humility in the exercise of vast responsibility—these attributes aptly describe you, Mr. Prime Minister, a courageous advocate for peace. On your visit here three years ago, I was among those who were moved and inspired by your vision of the common interest of young Israelis and young Arabs in peace. You reminded us that the young people of the Middle East must reject the bitterness of their ancestors and turn toward each other to live in harmony. Yours was a beautiful vision—involving a passion for justice, compassion for all things human, and humility. I am glad you have returned to teach us once again.

Blessed Is the Match

The main camp at Auschwitz was situated not in remote isolation but in a densely populated region. To the east, immediately adjacent to the camp, was a pleasant village, complete with a hotel and shops, built to house SS troops and their families. One mile farther east was the town of Auschwitz, intended by the very men who ordered the construction of the camps to be a center of industrial activity, a focus of German resettlement at the confluence of three rivers, with easy access to the coal fields of Upper Silesia.[1]

In his chilling work on the origins of Auschwitz, Robert-Jan van Pelt documents the utopian vision that drove the systematic planning for German colonization of the East. In December 1941, Hans Strosberg, the architect and master planner, sent his friends a New Year's greeting card. On the front he wished them "health, happiness, and a good outcome for every new beginning." The card's central spread depicted his drawings for a reconstruction of the central marketplace in Auschwitz. The inscription on the back of the greeting

Keynote Address, "*Yom Hashoah:* Days of Remembrance," Rotunda of the U.S. Capitol, April 23, 1998

1. Robert-Jan van Pelt, "Auschwitz: From Architect's Promise to Inmate's Perdition," *Modernism/Modernity* 1, no. 1 (January 1994): 80–120. See also Debórah Dwork and Robert-Jan van Pelt, *Auschwitz: 1270 to the Present* (New York: W. W. Norton), 1996.

card connected Stosberg's current project with National Socialist mythology:

> In the year 1241 Silesian knights, acting as saviors of the Reich, warded off the Mongolian assault at Wahlstatt. In that same century Auschwitz was founded as a German town. After six hundred years [*sic*] the *Führer* Adolf Hitler is turning the Bolshevik menace away from Europe. This year, 1941, the construction of a new German city and the reconstruction of the old Silesian market have been planned and initiated.

To Stosberg's inscription I would add that during the same year, 1941, it was decided to reduce the space allocated to each prisoner at the nearby Auschwitz-Birkenau camp from 14 to 11 square feet.

How, in one of the most civilized nations on earth, could an architect boast about work that involved not only designing the handsome town center depicted on his greeting card but the meticulous planning of facilities to house the slave labor to build it?

This is but one of numberless questions that knowledge of the Holocaust compels us to ask. In the details of its horror the Holocaust forces us to redefine the range of human experience; it demands that we confront *real,* not imagined, experiences that defy imagination.

How can we begin to understand the dehumanizing loss of identity suffered by the victims in the camps? How can we begin to understand the insensate rationality and brutality of the persecutors? How can we begin to understand the silence of the bystanders? There is only one answer: by remembering.

The distinguished Yale scholar Geoffrey Hartman tells us that "the culture of remembrance is at high tide. . . . At present, three generations are preoccupied with Holocaust memory. There are the eyewitnesses; their children, the second generation, who have subdued some of their ambivalence and are eager to know their parents better; and the third generation, grandchildren who treasure the personal stories of relatives now slipping away."[2]

The tide will inevitably recede. And if there are no survivors to tell the story, who will make their successors remember and help them to understand?

Our educational institutions must shoulder this burden, and their efforts are already under way. The exhibitions and publications of the Holocaust Memorial Museum in Washington, along with those of sister museums in other cities, are educating the public about the horrors of the Shoah. Museums, university archives, and private foundations are collecting and preserving the materials that enable us to learn from the past, and it is the special role of universities to support the scholars who explore and illuminate this dark episode in human history. Our universities have a dual responsibility: to preserve the memory of the Holocaust and to seek a deeper understanding of it.

This is a daunting and important responsibility. To confront future generations with the memory of the Holocaust is to change forever their conception of humanity. To urge them to understand it is to ask their commitment to prevent its recurrence.

In the words of Hannah Senesh, the twenty-three-year-old poet and patriot executed as a prisoner of the Reich in Budapest, "Blessed is the match that is consumed in kindling a flame." May the act of remembrance consume our ignorance and indifference, and light the way to justice and righteousness.

2. Geoffrey Hartman, "Shoah and Intellectual Witness," *Partisan Review* no. 1 (1998): 37.

Reflections on the American Economy

Can America Compete in World Markets?

An Unconventional View of the 1980s

orty-eight years ago the United States emerged from war as
the dominant economic power in the world. For the first half
of the near half-century that followed, American industrial hegemony was unquestioned. Indeed, in 1968 a best-selling book entitled
The American Challenge aroused the fears of Europeans that their entire economies were on the verge of becoming mere subsidiaries of
large American-owned companies. The briefly famous book by Jean-
Jacques Servan-Schreiber created a tremendous furor in European
capitals. Pressures to increase the common external tariffs of the
fledgling European Community and to restrict American investment
were resisted, but only after considerable struggle.

The fears of an American takeover of Europe were of course
vastly exaggerated. American economic growth had been dramatic
from 1945 to 1968, but, starting from a position of leadership, it had
in fact been slower than that of every major economy in the industrialized world. In 1950, Japan's per capita gross domestic product was
one-sixth that of the United States'. Germany's was one-third, and
Britain's about three-fifths of our level. By 1968, Japan's per capita

A lecture to the New Haven League of Women Voters, February 3, 1993, based on
lessons learned teaching a Yale College course from 1988 to 1990 on "The Competitiveness of U.S. Manufacturing Industry"

GDP had grown to half our level, Germany's to 61 percent, and Britain's to 63 percent.

I recall this example of continental panic to suggest that current anxiety about our international competitors, and especially Japan, may be unwarranted. Indeed, that will be the central message of this lecture: despite our persistent trade deficits, despite the loss of jobs in the manufacturing sector, and despite our mounting national debt, America can and does compete effectively in the world economy.

To demonstrate this I want first to point briefly to the negative indicators that give cause for concern about the competitiveness of our economy: the trade deficit, the rise of direct foreign investment in the United States, and the loss of jobs in the manufacturing sector. I will focus throughout on the manufacturing sector both domestically and abroad, and in particular on the development of new technology in the manufacturing sector, for it is widely believed that the superiority of American technology created the hegemony that we enjoyed following World War II. I will argue that macroeconomic policy, not a lack of competitiveness, is primarily responsible for the trade deficit, increased foreign investment, and loss of jobs. I will then present some comparative international data to assess the overall strength of our manufacturing sector. To foreshadow the conclusion here, Japan is catching up, but we're still ahead and in fact gaining a bit of ground on the other advanced industrial countries. Then I will focus on a few technologically advanced sectors, where the news, despite some well-known problems in the electronics industries, is pretty good on balance. I will close by discussing some bad ideas and some good ideas for public policies designed to improve the competitive position of the U.S. economy.

Let's look at some bad news first. There was a small surplus in the balance of merchandise trade in the 1960s, with deficits of modest size from the mid-1970s to early 1980s. Then catastrophe occurred, if you believe what you read in the newspapers. In 1984 the deficit hit $100 billion, where it remained. There was a modest recovery in 1991, only to be followed by a return to deficits in the $100 billion plus range in 1992.

Not every American knows these numbers, but virtually every American is aware of some of their highly visible manifestations. The consumer electronics industry (TVs, VCRs, calculators, video games) is dominated by imports. More important, the domestic automobile industry, which remains the largest single employer in the manufacturing sector, has declined dramatically in the presence of intense foreign competition. Although the volume of imports has stabilized in recent years, the penetration of foreign brands continues to grow through the operation of "transplants"—foreign-owned manufacturing establishments based in the U.S.

This is another sign of trouble reminiscent of the earlier American Challenge: the rise of foreign direct investment in the United States. Between 1980 and 1990, the percentage of U.S. manufacturing assets owned by foreigners roughly doubled. More than five hundred manufacturing plants in the United States were acquired or opened by Japanese investors. About half were existing plants; the other half were grass-roots, newly built plants.

Finally, there is the loss of jobs in the manufacturing sector. From 1946 to 1969 the number of jobs in manufacturing grew steadily from 14 million to 20 million. Fluctuating cyclically in the 1970s, the number of manufacturing jobs was still 20 million in 1980. Now there are only 18 million. Twenty years ago, one-quarter of U.S. workers were in manufacturing; today only one-sixth are so engaged.

Should we interpret the trade deficit, the increased foreign direct investment, and the decline in manufacturing employment as evidence that our manufacturing industries cannot compete in world markets? I'm going to argue against drawing that conclusion. Let me first offer alternative interpretations of the data on the trade deficit, foreign investment, and manufacturing employment. Then I will discuss other indicators of our international competitive position.

First, consider the trade deficit. Staggering though it may seem, the trade deficit is less a reflection of our weakness in manufacturing than it is a manifestation of the fiscal policies of the Reagan-Bush era.

To oversimplify a complex set of connections, the deficit in our international trade balance is an artifact of the much larger deficit in the federal government's budget. Currently the budget deficit is in excess of $300 billion, which represents 5 percent of the GDP.

A deficit this size is historically unprecedented in peacetime. Indeed, it is unprecedented in all wars save one—the Second World War, when the federal deficit hit 30 percent of GDP. During the Korean War the deficit did not exceed 2.2 percent of GDP. At the height of the Vietnam War and at the peak of the OPEC-induced recession of the mid-'70s, the deficit briefly exceeded 3 percent of GDP. Otherwise, from 1947 through 1979 the deficit never exceeded 2.5 percent of GDP and was almost always below 1.6 percent. In dramatic contrast, in every year from 1983 to 1992 the deficit exceeded 3.5 percent of GDP, and in five of the ten years the deficit exceeded 5 percent.

Look at it another way. The size of the national debt—which is the accumulation of annual deficits of the federal government—was a little larger than GDP at the end of World War II. By 1964 economic growth and the oft-maligned tools of Keynesian fiscal policy had worked down the outstanding debt to less than half of GDP. In 1981, when Ronald Reagan came to office, the national debt was one-third of GDP. When George Bush left office, in 1993, it was nearly three-quarters of GDP.

While I am digressing into macroeconomics, I can't resist one more observation. The popular view of Reagan-Bush economics is that its main achievement was to cut our tax burden, which was excessively high. This view is false in two respects: the tax burden wasn't cut, and it wasn't excessively high. First, although there were substantial cuts in federal income taxes, especially for the top 2 to 5 percent of the income distribution, the aggregate cuts in the federal tax burden were offset by increases in state and local taxes—a lesson which we residents of New Haven and Connecticut have learned with a vengeance. Second, our tax burden is the lowest among the major industrialized countries. It has been lower than Europe's throughout the entire postwar period. It is now lower than Japan's.

What does all this have to do with the trade deficit? To oversimplify the macroeconomics, the government has to finance its deficit somehow. In the 1980s it sold bonds and treasury bills, attracting unprecedented volumes of foreign capital to the United States. During the second half of the 1980s, when the trade deficit rose above $100 billion annually, the flow of new foreign capital to the nation was just about double this level—exceeding $200 billion annually from 1986 through 1989. A capital influx of this magnitude augments the demand for dollars, tending to increase its value in relation to other currencies, lowering the price of imported goods to U.S. consumers and raising the price of U.S. goods to foreign consumers. Thus, the large federal deficits led to an influx of foreign capital, which increased our demand for imports and reduced the foreign demand for our exports, thus increasing the trade deficit.

What about foreign direct investment—not in the paper assets of the U.S. Treasury but in manufacturing enterprises throughout the country? Is this a sign of competitive weakness or a threat to our future prosperity? First, although the growth of foreign direct investment has been rapid, the total share of U.S. manufacturing assets owned by foreigners remains small, less than 15 percent. The Japanese, whose investments seem to arouse the most concern, still own less than 1.5 percent of U.S. manufacturing assets. Second, much of the recent activity has been in direct response to restrictive U.S. trade policies—specifically import quotas. This is most striking in the automobile industry, where the Japanese have made more than half their investments—in direct and explicit response to the so-called voluntary quotas negotiated on the export of Japanese-made vehicles to the United States. In other words, a considerable portion of the increase in foreign direct investment is the result of our own attempts to keep foreign-made goods out. Although all trade restrictions are costly in the long run to worldwide economic growth and prosperity, this particular one at least had the virtue of creating some domestic employment in manufacturing.

Finally, what about the overall decline in manufacturing jobs?

This, too, is not so clearly a sign of weakness as it may seem on the surface. Recall that industrial development was initially stimulated by rapid productivity growth in agriculture, which allowed a shrinking number of agricultural workers to provide food to a growing urban-industrial population. That was the dominant dynamic of economic development from the mid-nineteenth to mid-twentieth century. In the past twenty to thirty years we have begun to see a pattern across all industrialized countries, whereby high productivity growth in manufacturing is releasing labor to the service sector. In the services, output growth is rapid (because the relative demand for services rises with income), and productivity growth is slower. Thus, a declining percentage of total employment in manufacturing is not unique to the U.S. The tendency to decline is less marked in Japan, and our percentage of employment in manufacturing is lower than elsewhere, but one reasonable interpretation of this picture is that we are a richer economy, with higher per capita incomes and a more developed service sector. We are just ahead of the other advanced countries in what is an inevitable evolution of jobs out of manufacturing.

How can we summarize the overall performance of our manufacturing sector? First, in the 1980s, despite the mounting trade deficit, U.S. industrial production grew faster than that of all our leading competitors save the Japanese. This superior performance was driven by an acceleration of productivity growth—partly the result of a shift in the pattern of output to more rapidly developing industries, partly the result of better performance within specific industries. Second, our level of manufacturing productivity remains the highest in the world. In constant 1980 dollars, output per labor-hour was about $20 in 1989 (or $28 to $29 in 1989 dollars); it was $15 in Japan and Germany, $10 in Britain. Third, over a thirty-year period, the gap among leading industrialized nations has decreased. The productivity of the United States was three times that of Germany and five times that of Japan in 1960; now it's just 33 percent higher. Fourth, although the Japanese continue to catch up, we gained ground on our European competitors in the 1980s, widening the gap between the United States and Germany during the past decade.

Let me turn now to an assessment of some specific manufacturing industries. Again, the bad news is well known. International competition has dramatically weakened the mature industries of the Rust Belt: the automobile industry and its once-principal material supplier, the steel industry. The decline in steel began in the 1960s; the automobile industry began its decline in the 1970s. I won't repeat these well-told stories: high labor costs played an important role here, as did the shortsightedness of management. Our industries failed to adjust quickly to new technologies in steel and to the changes in automobile demand induced by the two OPEC oil price shocks. The decline of these sectors was particularly visible for two reasons: they accounted for lots of jobs, and the jobs were concentrated in one region of the country.

The real strength of American manufacturing since 1960 has been in the science-based, technology-intensive industries: chemicals, pharmaceuticals, computers and other electronic equipment, aircraft and instruments. Yet some observers of these so-called high-tech industries fear that even in this sector of the economy American leadership is waning.

First, there is grave concern that interventionist policies in Japan and elsewhere have given various national industries an unfair advantage in international competition. The Japanese domestic market has been protected from U.S. imports in many sectors, and this denial of access has had some impact on our international position. A somewhat more dubious charge is that the success of the Japanese in electronics has been the result of concerted policy, orchestrated by government, to dominate world markets. The Japanese government, through MITI (the Ministry of International Trade and Industry), has mounted numerous programs of industrial cooperation and employed various subsidies to promote Japanese firms. I'll come back to this.

Second, some direct measures of technological achievement suggest cause for concern. For example, although the number of patents filed is a pretty crude index of a nation's technological condition, patents do reflect, somewhat imperfectly, where new ideas are coming from. In the late 1960s, U.S. inventors filed 75 percent of all patent applications in the U.S. By the early 1980s, U.S. nationals filed only 60 percent of U.S. applications; by 1990, it was only 55 percent.

On close examination, however, the situation in high-tech industries lends little support to those who fear collapse is imminent. Despite a staggering $100 billion deficit in merchandise trade overall, most high-tech sectors had positive trade balances in 1990. It's true that the Japanese had a larger high-tech surplus, but ours was well ahead of any other advanced nation's.

The picture is augmented by data on our world market share in high-technology products. The Japanese have passed us in electronics, computers, and communications equipment (this category includes final products like VCRs, TVs, and cellular phones, as well as electronic components like microchips). But the United States remains a strong second in those fields and leads in all the others—by a commanding margin in chemicals, industrial engines and turbines, and especially in aircraft and instruments.

Finally, we should consider again the patent data, focusing on the propensity of citizens and corporations of the leading industrial countries to file patent applications outside their home markets. Despite the increase in foreign patenting in the United Sates, this country remains by far the largest source of external patent applications. In 1988 we filed twice as many patents outside our home market as the Japanese. The gap is closing—we filed three times the Japanese total ten years earlier—but it is still substantial. We still lead the world in new ideas.

The next question is obviously this: although we remain ahead in manufacturing productivity and in the development of new technology, won't we inevitably lose our lead? Although there is a long-run tendency for economies to converge as they develop, let me give three reasons why we are likely to remain in front for at least a while.

First, government programs to promote specific industries, such as those introduced by Japan's MITI, work better for catching up than for maintaining leadership. In the 1970s, government programs to promote the electronics industry in Japan had specific objectives that were known to be attainable. It is less often noted that the Japanese government's programs in the 1980s—specifically efforts in supercomputing and artificial intelligence—were dramatic failures. The goal of these programs was not merely to catch up but to achieve world technological leadership, to extend the frontier of usable knowledge. Despite substantial efforts the Japanese remain far behind the United States in these targeted areas of technology.

Second, the U.S. is far ahead in those areas of industrial technology that are most closely linked to advances in basic science. Most notably, America holds a commanding international position in biomedical technology. Although the recession has slowed developments in this field, the opportunities remain staggering and we have a formidable lead.

Third, the U.S. science infrastructure is absolutely dominant. Our basic research enterprise, which lagged behind Germany's before the Second World War, was built through the far-sighted policy of public support for university-based science articulated during the Truman administration and pursued consistently, though with varying intensity, ever since. This highly successful policy rested on the premise that strength in basic science would be a source of both military security and industrial growth. A unique feature of the American approach to basic science was to locate its center of gravity within universities rather than national laboratories or research institutes, thus ensuring a dual commitment to research and teaching, to the advancement of knowledge and the reproduction of a national capacity for continued scientific advance. A supposed sign of our industrial weakness is the frequently recited claim that Japan has seven engineers for every lawyer and we have seven lawyers for every engineer. (Incidentally, the claim is false. We actually have more than two engineers for every lawyer.) Japan, however, has three engineers for every scientist. We have more scientists than engineers.

Next, I promised to comment on some bad ideas and some good ideas for public policy. Some bad ideas:

First among these is protection. Because our economy is large, our national interest is ultimately well served by policies of free and open trade that promote global economic growth. As a large exporter and importer, we have much to lose from trade war. Moreover, keeping Japanese products out of the United States won't necessarily strengthen our firms in other markets. Protection insulates domestic firms from competitive pressure, reducing their incentives to lower cost and increase productivity. This is a step backward. American firms need to be exposed to the rigors of international competition. They can succeed, especially in industries based on advanced technology.

A second bad idea: abolish or further weaken the antitrust laws. This is a terrible idea, but one that tempts many businessmen. The competitive market system has spurred innovation. Competition provides the incentive to develop new ideas; it provides the carrot to the successful and the stick of discipline to the unsuccessful. The current enthusiasm for domestic collaboration and collusion in the face of foreign competition should be resisted. In an impressive study of one hundred firms that are world leaders in their particular market segments or industries, the Harvard economist Michael Porter found that in virtually no case did these highly successful firms owe their success to cooperative arrangements with competitors, and very few indeed had grown through mergers and acquisitions of competitors. Almost all made it by winning a competitive struggle, growing by internal expansion, not acquisition.

A third bad idea: targeting industries for government support and subsidies. It's costly and has no proven track record in the U.S. economy, where government and business are more adversarial than in Japan. And even if a new era of cooperation were to dawn, there is another problem. Targeting may work for catch up, but it is unlikely to guide innovation, as we have seen with the Japanese experience during the past decade. It takes many bad ideas to generate one good one. Government programs have a disastrous tendency to put too many eggs in one basket, while the market encourages a diversity of approaches and selects the best for reward and profit.

Finally, here are two good ideas.

First, secure access to foreign markets. Protectionism shrinks the international pie. The United States must persuade others to take this global view and resist powerful domestic industries desirous of short-term gain. A positive feature of the trade policy pursued by the Bush administration was its emphasis on negotiating the opening of foreign markets to U.S. products. This approach, however, should be used with caution; if it leads to sanctions and reprisals, it can be a dangerous game.

Second, support basic science. For the past twenty years, the United States has been the source of 35 percent of all scientific publications worldwide. Half of all students worldwide who leave their countries for study abroad come to this country. In itself, and because of the benefits it transmits to our high-tech industries, our university-based scientific enterprise is an essential source of our comparative advantage. The long-run persistence of this precious advantage is currently threatened, however, not by international competition but by shortsighted public policy.

I make this last claim not as a self-interested university administrator concerned about cutbacks in federal funding of university research, but as an industrial economist concerned about the strength of the national economy. The Reagan and Bush administrations have shifted the balance of federal funding away from basic research and toward research with more visible and immediate industrial application. This is a serious mistake, for at least four reasons. First, despite a few notable exceptions (the space station and super-collider programs), basic research tends to be much cheaper than applied research and product development. Second, the market performs much better than the government in selecting among areas of applied research. Third, basic research is less likely to be adequately supported by the private sector than is applied research and development, because the output of basic research is hard to appropriate directly for private benefit. Thus, the private sector will tend to underinvest in basic research. But it is much easier to reap the returns from applied research, and it will therefore tend to get done by the private sector without substantial government subsidy. Finally, basic research, undertaken primarily in our universities, is the source from which all applied research and development ultimately flows. Basic science renews the pool of opportunities for improvement in technology. For all these reasons, the appropriate role for government is to provide the funds to keep science advancing. If we can count on the government to foster an environment of rapid scientific progress, we can rely on the market to provide the incentive for U.S. firms to maintain their competitive edge.

Democracy and the Market

T he robust condition of industry and commerce in the fledgling American democracy was not lost on its most perceptive
visitor and ethnographer. Alexis de Tocqueville wrote:

The United States has only been emancipated for half a
century from the state of colonial dependence in which it
stood to Great Britain; the number of large fortunes there
is small and capital is still scarce. Yet no people in the
world have made such rapid progress in trade and manu-
factures as the Americans. . . .
. . . [T]hey have already changed the whole order of
nature for their own advantage.[1]

For Tocqueville, the robust condition of private enterprise in
America depended on the abundance of land, the absence of hereditary aristocracy, and, significantly, the presence of democratic institutions and egalitarian values. But Tocqueville foresaw the possibility
that the growth of commerce and manufacturing might create a new
aristocracy, which might in turn undermine the very democratic values that initially stimulated American economic development. Today,
as if to prove that free expression survives, some believe that Tocque-

One of the Tercentennial DeVane Lectures in the series "Democratic Vistas," February 6,
2001

1. Alexis de Tocqueville, *Democracy in America* (New York: Vintage, 1945), volume 2,
pp. 165–166.

ville's prediction has come true, that the market has subverted our democracy, while others believe that the free market is an essential safeguard against the erosion of democratic values.

How should we understand the relationship of the market economy and American democracy? Does a developed market economy encourage or discourage democratic values and institutions? And to the extent that an unfettered market economy creates forces inimical to democratic values, how can these forces be most effectively—one might even say, economically—countered?

These are the questions I address in this essay. First, I characterize the essential properties of the market economy. Then I comment on how the market economy both supports in part and undermines in part the central values of a democratic society. Finally, I describe how collective action through democratic government can, in principle, temper the antidemocratic consequences of market forces. I note that, in practice, political intervention in the market often promotes one democratic value, typically equality, over both economic efficiency and another democratic value, individual freedom. I conclude by suggesting how public intervention in markets might be structured to achieve greater equality of opportunity or outcomes at minimal sacrifice of economic efficiency or freedom.

Although both market economies and democracies take varied forms around the world, my principal subject is the relationship between the distinctively *American* market economy and *American* democracy. Where I depart from the abstract and general, it is the American example that I have in mind.

There is no better starting point than Adam Smith's enduring classic *The Wealth of Nations,* especially his opening chapters and discussion of international trade.[2] Nowhere else will you find the essential features of a market economy so elegantly described.

2. Adam Smith, *An Inquiry into the Nature and Causes of the Wealth of Nations* (Chicago: University of Chicago Press, 1976), Book I, chapters 1–3, and Book IV, chapter 2.

Smith asserts that "the propensity to truck, barter, and exchange one thing for another" is common to all humans possessed with the faculties of reason and speech.[3] But we need not rely on Smith's anthropology to recognize that voluntary exchange is at the center, both logically and historically, of the development of the market economy. Voluntary exchange depends on the decisions of autonomous individuals. Each party to a transaction decides: I willingly surrender what I have for what you offer in exchange. Exchange improves the position of both parties.

Smith develops the benign implications of this insight. We need not rely on the altruism of our trading partner. Each of us can pursue our independent self-interest and gain from trade. In Smith's famous formulation, "it is not from the benevolence of the butcher, the brewer, or the baker that we expect our dinner, but from their regard to their own interest. We address ourselves, not to their humanity but to their self-love, and never talk to them of our own necessities but of their advantage."[4]

The pursuit of self-interest has broader implications for the society as a whole. Consider this argument of Smith's concerning the allocation of capital, an argument that could be made equally well with regard to the allocation of labor: "Every individual is continually exerting himself to find out the most advantageous employment for whatever capital he can command. It is his own advantage, indeed, and not that of the society which he has in view. But the study of his own advantage naturally, or rather necessarily leads him to prefer that employment which is most advantageous to society."[5]

Smith continues: "It is only for the sake of profit that any man employs a capital in support of industry; and he will always, therefore, endeavor to employ it in the support of that industry of which the produce is likely to be of the greatest value."[6]

3. Ibid., p. 17.
4. Ibid., p. 18.
5. Ibid., p. 475.
6. Ibid., p. 477.

By thus pursuing profit, in Smith's account: "Every individual necessarily labours to render the annual revenue of society as great as he can. . . . He intends only his own gain, and he is in this, as in many other cases, led by an invisible hand to promote an end which was no part of his intention."[7]

Smith's conclusion that an individual will allocate capital, or indeed his own labor, to the use that he values most highly follows directly from the assumption that the individual rationally pursues his self-interest. But the conclusion that total social benefit (in Smith's words the "annual revenue of society") will be thereby maximized requires more assumptions than are made explicit in the famous "invisible hand" passage.

Indeed, it was more than a century after publication of *The Wealth of Nations* that neo-classical economists worked out the precise conditions required to show that decentralized decisions by self-interested individuals produce a socially beneficial result. Most important of these additional assumptions is that every individual, in calculating the best use of his resources, faces a common set of prices for goods or services; in other words, we need market prices that signal a common social valuation. No person or business enterprise can have the power to influence these prices, ruling out monopoly. And no good or service that creates utility for the individual or profit for the enterprise can be unpriced, ruling out the presence of externalities or missing markets. Finally, in the neo-classical analysis of Smith's invisible hand conjecture, the world is strictly static. That is, the resources available to each individual (labor, capital, and land) are fixed, as is the technology of transforming those resources into useful products.

These conditions, along with a couple of technical ones, assure that the market economy allocates resources efficiently, in the sense first defined by Vilfredo Pareto. That is to say, no individual can be made better off without making another worse off. This tendency to

7. Ibid.

allocate a society's productive resources efficiently is one of the two most important advantages of a market economy.

Curiously, although the neo-classical economists focused almost exclusively on making rigorous this insight of Adam Smith, efficient resource allocation was not the central concern of his great treatise. Instead, Smith focused on a larger question: what explains the differences in economic progress and material well-being among nations? The answer to this question is given in the first three chapters of Book I of *The Wealth of Nations* and elaborated throughout the treatise. Progress in material well-being depends most significantly on the advantages derived from ever-increasing specialization in production, which Smith calls the division of labor.

Smith observes that specialization depends on the possibility of exchange, which frees the individual from self-sufficiency. He identifies three types of advantages from specialization: increased skill at a specific trade or subdivision of that trade, savings from eliminating movement from one activity to another, and the possibility of vast increases in productivity through mechanization. Smith recognizes that these potential benefits from the division of labor provide an incentive to innovate for both the worker on the job and the "philosopher," which is Smith's quaintly dignified way of describing what we today would call an inventor or entrepreneur. Workers and so-called philosophers alike thus have two powerful incentives arising from their self-interested pursuit of material well-being: first, to reallocate labor and capital from lower to higher valued uses (given the existing technology of production), and second, to seek out new and improved technologies that increase society's productive capacity.

Differences in material well-being, according to Smith, depend on the extent to which nations have taken advantage of the potential benefits of the division of labor. And their capacity to do so depends on the extent of the market. The logic of this observation is simple: the benefit to be derived from a new piece of textile machinery, for example, depends on the size of the market for textiles. Some nations enjoy natural advantages from large populations and proximity to water transport, both of which create large potential markets.

Smith focuses much of his treatise on the policies of governments that inhibit the scope of exchange and the size of the market and thereby limit the potential gains from new technology and the progress of material well-being. Over the past 225 years others have added refinements to his arguments against protective tariffs and inefficient forms of taxation, but Smith got the essential points right.

Among twentieth-century economists, who principally chose to work on problems of static resource allocation, Joseph Schumpeter stands out as the most spirited defender of the true Smithian tradition. He first articulates a view of capitalist development in his 1912 book, *The Theory of Economic Development*. But his most succinct argument for identifying dynamic rather than static efficiency as the central advantage of a market economy is given in chapter 7 of *Capitalism, Socialism, and Democracy*, written during the Second World War. Here he rails against those who denounce capitalism on the grounds that monopolistic and oligopolistic firms distort the allocation of resources away from the competitive, statically efficient, outcome. Instead, he observes that the market economy is dynamic and evolutionary in its nature—that the technology and organization of production, as well as the nature of products themselves, is constantly changing. To evaluate an economy's performance simply with reference to static efficiency criteria is to miss the most important measure of economic performance—the rate at which material well-being is increasing.

To Schumpeter, the competition that matters is not competition to win customers within an existing market, but competition for "the new commodity, the new technology, the new source of supply, the new type of organization."[8] This process of "creative destruction" shapes the economy in far more profound ways than any competition

8. Joseph A. Schumpeter, *Capitalism, Socialism, and Democracy*, 3rd ed. (New York: Harper, 1950), p. 84.

within existing markets; it also produces advances in productivity and material well-being far in excess of the benefits attributable to the efficient allocation of existing resources. For example, most credible empirical estimates, crude as they are, of the economic losses from inefficient resource allocation range from less than 1 to about 2 percent of a fixed national product.[9] Yet the benefits from new technologies and new products might be conservatively reckoned to increase per capita national product by as much as 1 or 2 percent *per year*.

We have just described the two principal advantages of a market economy—its tendency toward efficient resource allocation and its tendency to foster innovation. We are now prepared to ask whether the workings of the market economy are favorable or inimical to the existence and survival of democracy. But first let us pause to consider briefly what the market requires from the political order in which it is embedded.

The answer to this preliminary question is pretty simple. The market rests on a foundation of voluntary exchange among self-interested individuals and the incentives that the possibility of voluntary exchange creates. For such a system to function, property rights must be well defined (I cannot trade what I do not own), and contracts, agreements among the parties to an exchange, must be enforceable. So the simple answer, as spelled out a century ago by Max Weber, is that markets require a rule of law—which entails both well-defined rules and a system to enforce those rules.[10] As a logical proposition, markets do not require democratic governments, only a stable and predictable rule of law, which, in theory, can exist in an authoritarian regime. France under Napoleon comes to mind. But, as an empirical proposition, markets have performed best in democratic regimes.

9. For a review of these estimates, see F. M. Scherer and David Ross, *Industrial Market Structure and Economic Performance,* 3rd ed. (Boston: Houghton Mifflin, 1990), pp. 661–667.
10. See especially Max Weber, *Economy and Society* (New York: Bedminster, 1968), volume 1, pp. 311–338.

Accepting the view that political order is good for the market, let us now ask if the market is good for democracy. I want to address this question by focusing on the two central values of American democracy—freedom and equality. Because the connection is so manifestly self-evident, I pass quickly over the relationship between the market and one additional defining characteristic of American democracy noted by Tocqueville and favored by Emerson and Whitman—self-reliance. This characteristic American virtue is intrinsic in Smith's philosopher-entrepreneur—the rational actor who seizes every opportunity to maximize the value of his resources. There can be little doubt that the market, with the incentives it provides to the alert and reflective, promotes self-reliance. By the same logic, the market promotes self-invention, which Anthony Kronman describes as the quintessential aspiration of the democratic soul.

Less obviously, the relationship between the market economy and political freedom is entirely symbiotic; the health of one promotes the health of the other. In contrast, the relationship of the market economy and equality is much more problematic. On the one hand, the market provides for radical equality of opportunity, but on the other hand markets are indifferent to equality of outcomes. Depending on technology and other exogenous factors, markets can increase or decrease equality in the distribution of income and wealth.

I have already noted that voluntary exchange is logically and historically at the center of the market economy. In theory, individuals have complete freedom—to offer labor services where they choose, to employ capital in a preferred use, to invest in education and training, to purchase food, shelter, clothing, and other consumption goods as they wish. In practice, freedom of action is constrained by the resources available to the individual; it is in this sense that prosperity expands our freedom. Still, within the limits of their resources, individuals are free agents in the market economy. They alone choose where to live, where to work, and what to eat. One need only look at the experience of the Soviet Union from the 1920s through the mid-1980s—where residences and occupations were assigned and food was frequently rationed—to recognize that such freedom has not been universal, even in modern times.

The freedom of action inherent in market activity supports and reinforces freedom in other spheres of life. If we can choose our occupation by selling labor services in the market, should we not be free to choose, subject to appropriate entry standards, the course of study we pursue in publicly supported educational institutions? If we are free to purchase books, magazines, newspapers, and cable television programming as we wish, should sellers not be free to publish opinions of any kind? Indeed, should we not be free to express our own opinions? My point is simply this: our freedom in the marketplace accustoms us to expect freedom in the political and social realm.

Milton Friedman offers another reason why economic freedom is conducive to political freedom.[11] In the market economy, the decentralization of decision-making tends to distribute power widely; there are more than two hundred billionaires, several million millionaires, and hundreds of very large, powerful corporations in America. In the political realm, however, power is more concentrated. Potentially, the leader of the state, even if democratically elected, has immense coercive power that is unavailable to economic agents who must compete in the marketplace. Thus, Friedman claims that the dispersed sources of power created by the market economy act as a check and balance against excessive exercise of the state's power to coerce. No doubt Friedman exaggerates the state's power to coerce by failing to acknowledge, on the one hand, that political power in our democracy is not in fact concentrated in a single leader and, on the other, that actions of the state can be enabling instead of coercive. Still, there is something to the argument that having a nonpolitical mechanism, the market, distribute power may help to preserve freedom better than a regime in which all power is created and distributed through political processes.

11. Milton Friedman, *Capitalism and Freedom*, 2nd ed. (Chicago: University of Chicago Press, 1982), pp. 15–19.

The relationship of the market to equality, the other principal democratic value, is less felicitous. On the one hand, just as the market promotes freedom, it creates a radical equality of opportunity. In principle, any individual with a good idea and access to capital can reap rewards in Schumpeterian competition. Historically, access to capital may have been limited on grounds of race and gender, but capital (especially in the form of credit) has always been widely available to American farmers and small businesses, whether start-ups or family firms of long standing. Although in the aggregate there has been no systematic tendency toward income equality in the past century, individual mobility, from one income level to another, from one social class to another, has been persistently high throughout American history.[12] One interesting piece of evidence: of the 400 wealthiest Americans identified annually by *Forbes* magazine, only one-third inherited their wealth or built their fortunes on a nucleus of inherited wealth.[13]

Now we come to the most disconcerting consequence of the market economy. In the process of economic growth through "creative destruction," the market creates losers as well as winners. In dynamic competition, the race goes to the swift, and many are left behind.

The data yield three robust conclusions. First, there is significant inequality in income and wealth among Americans. Second, during the course of the twentieth century the extent of inequality fluctuated; there was no systematic tendency toward either increased

12. Peter Gottschalk and Sheldon Danzinger, "Family Income Mobility—How Much Is There and Has It Changed," Boston College, Department of Economics Working Paper #398, December 1997. Much empirical work on the subject of mobility is, in my view, conceptually flawed. The typical studies of mobility look at an individual's movement from one income class to another. But it is well known that income tends first to rise and then fall throughout the life cycle of most individuals. We need studies that control for these life-cycle effects or, better still, finesse them entirely by looking at intergenerational mobility, rather than an individual's progress from year to year or decade to decade.
13. *Forbes,* October 9, 2000, p. 362.

or decreased inequality. Third, inequality has increased significantly since the early 1980s.

Let's begin with the current extent of inequality. In the mid-1990s, the top 5 percent of families received just over 20 percent of all pre-tax family income;[14] the top 0.5 percent of families received just under 10 percent of all such income.[15] To give these figures some life, consider a random sample of 200 American families. On average, the ten highest-income families (that is, the top 5 percent of the sample) would earn average incomes of $172,000, almost five times larger than those of the other 190 families (roughly $36,000). The top family alone, in any random sample of 200, would, on average, have an income of $860,000, nine times the average income of the next nine families ($96,000), or twenty-four times the $36,000 average income of the bottom 190 families. Household wealth—the value of stocks, bonds, real estate, and other assets—is even more unequally distributed. In 1995, the top 1 percent held 38 percent of all wealth; the top 5 percent held 60 percent.[16]

Over the course of the twentieth century there was no sustained trend in inequality, but rather fluctuations. Curiously, these fluctuations display no consistent correlation with the overall growth in incomes. Sometimes big boats get greater lift from a rising tide; sometimes the small boats rise the most.

To summarize, the share of family income going to the top 5 percent of families was 23 percent just after the First World War. It rose during the prosperity of the 1920s to a peak of 26 percent

14. The calculation is based on pre-tax income, excluding capital gains. Nonmonetary income—such as employer-provided health benefits, Medicare, Medicaid, and food stamps—is also excluded. Frank Levy, *The New Dollars and Dreams* (New York: Sage Foundation, 1998), pp. 199, 203.

15. This calculation is based on standardized pre-tax adjusted gross income, excluding capital gains. See Daniel R. Feenberg and James M. Poterba, "The Income and Tax Share of Very-High Income Households, 1960–1995," *American Economic Review* 90, no. 2 (May 2000): 264–270.

16. Edward N. Wolff, "Recent Trends in the Distribution of Household Wealth," *Journal of Economic Perspectives* 12, no. 3 (Summer 1998): 136.

(1928–32), then fell during the Depression years to reach 23 percent again on the eve of the Second World War (1939–40).[17] In contrast to the boom of the 1920s, the boom induced by the Second World War led to greater equality. By 1947 the top 5 percent of families had only 17.5 percent of family income. The share of the richest families fell gradually throughout the entire era of postwar growth, to about 15 percent, and it did not increase during the slump of the 1970s. As the stock market recovered in the 1980s preceding the acceleration of overall economic growth in the 1990s, income inequality began to rise again, with the share of the top 5 percent of families reaching 18 percent by 1989 and topping 20 percent by 1996.[18] It is particularly alarming that the share of income going to the very richest families has risen dramatically in recent years. The share going to the top 0.5 percent fluctuated between 5 and 6 percent of total family income from 1960 to 1982. Thereafter, it has risen precipitously to between 9 and 10 percent in every year since 1988.[19]

Many factors have contributed to fluctuations in the extent of inequality. At the risk of oversimplification, I would suggest that the gradual reduction in inequality between 1945 and 1970 was probably most significantly influenced by the movement of lower-income farmers and farm workers to higher-paying urban jobs. Underlying this change in the distribution of jobs, however, were steady increases in agricultural productivity and rapid growth in the production of automobiles, which created a derived demand for materials used in the production of automobiles, such as steel, as well as demand for com-

17. Simon Kuznets, *Shares of Upper Income Groups in Income and Savings* (New York: National Bureau of Economic Research, 1953), p. 585.
18. The data covering 1947 through 1995 are drawn from Levy, *New Dollars*, p. 199. Levy and Kuznets use different methods for calculating and ranking family incomes. Thus, the direction of movement in the pre-war and postwar data is accurately portrayed, but the pre-war income shares of the top 5 percent should not be directly compared to the post-war shares. Where the data overlap, however, in 1947, the share calculated by Kuznets is only 0.1 percent lower than Levy's.
19. Feenberg and Poterba, "Income and Tax Share of Very-High Income Households."

plementary products, such as gasoline. It is sometimes asserted that the Interstate Highway Act of 1956 was the most important piece of post–World War II social legislation because it suburbanized our cities, altered the relationship of home and workplace, and restructured the use of leisure time. It may also have reduced inequality in the distribution of income.

By contrast to this somewhat speculative inference, the factors contributing to increasing inequality over the past two decades have been intensively studied. It is widely agreed that the most important source of rising inequality is technological change that has significantly increased the premium paid for highly educated, skilled workers. In fact, the wage premium earned by those with a college degree rose from 31 percent to 53 percent between 1979 and 1993, even as the proportion of workers with a college degree increased from 22 percent to 29 percent.[20] It should not be surprising that the rise in the relative pay of educated workers began just as the personal computer was introduced. Empirical investigation confirms that the premium paid for educated workers is highest in precisely those industries making the most intensive use of computers.[21]

We have now examined, on the positive side, the market's reinforcement of democratic freedoms and its tendency to create opportunity for upward mobility. On the negative side, we find that market forces have caused increases in the inequality of income and wealth over the past two decades. Excessive inequality threatens the philosophical basis of democracy, which counts each individual as an autonomous agent capable of self-invention.

Our American democracy appears willing to tolerate a substantial degree of inequality, but we have nonetheless used political

20. Peter Gottschalk, "Inequality, Income Growth, and Mobility: The Basic Facts," *Journal of Economic Perspectives* 11, no. 2 (Spring 1997): 29–31.
21. See David H. Autor, Lawrence F. Katz, and Alan B. Krueger, "Computing Inequality: Have Computers Changed the Labor Market?" *Quarterly Journal of Economics* 113, no. 4 (November 1998): 1169–1213.

means, acts of government, to temper the tendency to inequality that market forces produce. I will shortly discuss efforts to equalize incomes through progressive taxation and various welfare programs. But first we should note that inequality of income and wealth is only one of many consequences of market activity that might be viewed as adverse by a majority of citizens. Excessive air and water pollution, insufficient workplace and product safety, and the use of child labor come to mind as additional examples.

Therefore, I want to examine how politically undesirable aspects and outcomes of market activity are controlled. In practice, many adverse consequences of market activity are prevented or meliorated by systems of industrial self-regulation. The financial and cost-accounting standards used by corporations and even nonprofit organizations are a notable example of self-regulation, as are various codes of conduct adopted by industry associations. But I set this subject aside to focus instead upon the action of government to ban, regulate, discourage, or otherwise constrain politically undesirable market processes and outcomes.

In our democracy, governmental intervention in markets is not rare; we do it all the time, with many different political objectives in mind. We intervene by prohibiting market activity in some cases, by taxing and subsidizing, and by promulgating and enforcing vast numbers of regulations regarding health, safety, environmental quality, information disclosure, employment conditions, and workers' rights—to give a very incomplete summary. Our interventions are not usually structured to ensure the best possible economic performance; efficiency is usually sacrificed in favor of political objectives. Our interventions are sometimes corrosive of important democratic values as well, such as personal freedom and self-reliance. Still, it is possible in principle to design, though not always possible in practice to achieve, interventions in the service of democratically determined political objectives that rely strongly on economic incentives to achieve their goals. Such interventions, if well conceived, can both minimize inefficiency and preserve a significant degree of freedom and self-reliance.

Consider the most drastic form of government intervention in the market—the prohibition of trade. We prohibit the sale of goods presumed to be harmful, such as narcotics, dangerous toys, and untested pharmaceuticals. We also prohibit the sale of universally distributed entitlements, such as the right to vote, the right to trial by jury, the right to marry one and only one spouse, and the right to public education, as well as police and fire protection services.

Prohibiting the trading of rights inhibits the personal freedom of both buyer and seller, and it is economically inefficient. We do not allow an individual to sell her right to vote to another person, even if the second person's willingness to pay far exceeds the minimum price the seller would accept. Under such circumstances, both parties would be better off by trading. The seller presumably would not sell unless she valued the cash more highly than her right to vote, and the buyer would not buy unless she valued having a second vote more highly than the dollars paid for it.

Presumably, we bar the trading of votes because in the political domain we collectively assign absolute primacy to equality. Although we tolerate what many believe to be excessive expenditures to influence voting, we hold sacrosanct the principle that each citizen's right and responsibility to participate in collective decision-making is inalienable. We insist upon one person, one vote even at the cost of reduced freedom and economic inefficiency.

I digress briefly to note that most other prohibitions of trade are not so easily explained by reference to almost universally shared values. These prohibitions reflect instead the will of a political majority. We typically recognize that there are competing values involved, and we differ on how heavily we weigh the loss of personal freedom and economic efficiency that prohibition entails. Consider the current prohibitions on the sale of tobacco to minors; marijuana; pharmaceuticals approved and marketed in Europe but not yet cleared by the U.S. Food and Drug Administration; and alcoholic beverages to individuals between the ages of eighteen and twenty-one. In each of these cases prohibition has costs and benefits. I would conjecture that many Americans favor one or more of these prohibitions and oppose one or more. On the other hand, I would be surprised if many believed that we should permit the buying and selling of votes.

Declaring certain entitlements universal and banning market transactions in them is only one of the approaches available to a democratic government seeking to compensate for the market's disregard for equality. We can also reduce inequality by levying taxes and awarding subsidies at rates that depend on income. We call a tax progressive when the ratio of tax payments to before-tax income rises with income. A progressive tax tends to equalize the distribution of income. We likewise call a subsidy progressive when the ratio of benefits to before-tax income falls as income rises. This, too, tends to render the distribution of income more equal.

Were the U.S. tax code designed simply to reduce inequality while raising revenue for the government, it would be a relatively efficient instrument for the purpose. In theory, high marginal tax rates reduce the incentive to work and thus reduce national output. In practice, however, changes in marginal tax rates in the range of recent U.S. experience have not had a substantial impact on labor supply, except in the case of those on welfare—an issue to which I will return. The major inefficiencies in the tax code arise from provisions that serve political objectives other than reducing inequality—such as encouraging home ownership and favoring certain types of investments and holding periods over others.

How well, then, do federal taxes serve the objective of reducing inequality? The answer has two parts. First, the federal income tax is highly progressive, and taken alone it would have a significant effect on inequality. The average taxpayer with less than $20,000 pays no taxes and receives a net subsidy. Taxpayers in the $20,000 to $30,000 income range pay only 2 percent on average, while those with incomes between $75,000 and $100,000 pay 11 percent and those with incomes above $200,000 pay 24 percent. Second, however, several other federal taxes on individuals are less progressive than the income tax. These include payroll taxes for Social Security and Medicare paid by every wage earner and employer, unemployment insurance for the self-employed, and excise taxes on various consumption goods, such as cigarettes and gasoline. The payroll tax that finances Social Security is actually regressive; there is no tax on income above $76,200. When all federal taxes are taken into account, the equalizing effects of the income tax are significantly attenuated. Average tax rates rise to 13 percent for incomes between $20,000 and $30,000, 23 percent for incomes between $75,000 and $100,000, and 28 percent for incomes above $200,000—still progressive, but much less progressive than the income tax alone.[22] This modest degree of overall progressivity in federal taxes reduces inequality, but not dramatically.[23]

In recent years, efforts to reduce inequality have focused on subsidizing those at the lower end of the income distribution rather than on taxing the rich. These subsidies take many forms—Medicaid, food stamps, housing allowances, job training programs, and cash payments. The long and complicated evolution of the many federal and state programs to assist the poor has reflected shifting views of both the causes and appropriate remedies for poverty. Some of the programs that were established or expanded in the 1960s, especially when taken in combination, created massive inefficiencies and horrendously perverse incentives for welfare recipients. Although recent legislation has been far from perfect, it has gone some distance toward providing constructive and efficiency-enhancing incentives for welfare recipients.

22. Joint Committee on Taxation, U.S. Congress, *Distribution of Certain Federal Tax Liabilities by Income Class for Calendar Year 2000* (JCX-45-00), April 11, 2000.
23. See Levy, *New Dollars,* pp. 205–208. Changes in the tax code in the 1980s and early 1990s have contained both progressive and regressive elements and have neither mitigated nor accentuated the trend toward greater inequality over the period. See Peter Gottschalk and Timothy Smeeding, "Cross-National Comparisons of Earnings and Income Inequality," *Journal of Economic Literature* 35, no. 2 (June 1997): 670.

Setting aside the elderly who are in poverty, and whose Social Security benefits are augmented by cash grants from the Supplemental Security Income program, the majority of welfare recipients are female heads of households, many of whom have children. Prior to the numerous reforms instituted by individual states in the 1980s, many of these single mothers received food stamps, subsidized housing, and cash grants from the Aid to Families with Dependent Children (AFDC) program. Eligibility for each of these programs was means-tested, and each used separate and distinct formulas to phase out benefits as the earned income of recipients increased. In many situations, the combined benefits lost when recipients entered employment exceeded the after-tax income from earnings. In other words, welfare recipients often faced marginal tax rates in excess of 100 percent. In other circumstances, the tax rate was below 100 percent but still very high, in excess of the marginal tax rates for the very highest income individuals in the nation. In fairness, not all welfare recipients faced such perverse incentives, but many did. And to the extent that those who did remained on welfare for protracted periods, their dependency might be more fairly represented as the pursuit of self-interest than as a moral failing. Intended to protect one democratic value— equality—our poorly designed welfare programs severely undermined another—self-reliance—while assessing an additional toll on economic efficiency.

The 1996 reform legislation sought to reduce dependency with both incentives and penalties.[24] Congress provided to the states two bloc grants to replace the AFDC cash grants to individuals and certain other child support programs. The first bloc of funds was for distribution to eligible recipients subject to two new requirements. First, to remain eligible for payments, able-bodied recipients must work at

24. For details on the recent reforms, see Committee on Ways and Means, U.S. House of Representatives, *Summary of Welfare Reforms Made by Public Law 104–193: The Personal Responsibility and Work Opportunity Reconciliation Act and Associated Legislation* (Washington, D.C.: U.S. Government Printing Office, November 6, 1996).

least part-time after two years on welfare. Second, recipients lose eligibility for payments after five years, although states can exempt up to 20 percent of their caseload from this provision. The other bloc grant represented a substantial increase in funds to subsidize the child care expenses of low-income working parents.

Enacted separately and often overlooked in the public discussion of welfare reform was a major improvement in the terms of the Earned Income Credit, a feature of the tax code first enacted in 1975.[25] The Earned Income Credit allows refunds against federal income taxes, calculated as a percentage of a taxpayer's first dollars of earned income. As income rises, the credit reaches a maximum at a certain threshold income. The credit then remains constant up to a second, higher-income threshold. Then the credit is phased out, diminishing gradually to zero at a third, higher level of income. The size of the credit was very small in the early years, not nearly large enough to adequately counter the perverse incentives faced by welfare recipients who sought work. But successive improvements in 1987, 1990, 1993, and 1996 changed the incentives substantially.

To illustrate, by the year 2000, a single mother with two children was allowed a 40 percent credit against the first $9,540 she earns each year, roughly the equivalent of working at the minimum wage for thirty-five hours a week. In such a situation, the wage earner would receive not only the $9,540 she earned but an additional $3,816 for a total of $13,356. Needless to say, this provides a substantial incentive for welfare recipients to take employment when it is available. In 2000, more than 18 million families received credits totaling $30 billion. Expenditures under this program now exceed cash payments under the AFDC and successor state programs, and they nearly equal the subsidy provided by food stamps.

The expansion of the Earned Income Credit to its current level was an important step toward making welfare reform efficient rather

25. For details, see Committee on Ways and Means, U.S. House of Representatives, *Green Book, 2000* (Washington, D.C.: U.S. Government Printing Office, 2000), pp. 808–813.

than punitive. But the program still has a major design flaw; the credit is phased out at a rate that is much too high. To continue with our hypothetical mother of two, for every dollar she earns in excess of $12,460, she would lose 21 cents of earned income credit, until no benefit remained. This phase-out provision, in combination with normal income and payroll taxes, creates an effective tax rate of 42.2 percent on earned income between $12,460 and $30,000. Eliminating the phase-out or spreading it over a much wider range of income would alter this perverse incentive.

Permit me a brief historical digression. If the Earned Income Credit were reformed as I just suggested, the program would resemble even more closely the negative income tax proposals advanced in the 1960s by both James Tobin on the left and Milton Friedman on the right.[26] The idea, when earnestly put forward by George McGovern in his 1972 presidential campaign, was ridiculed by his opponents as a "$1,000 giveaway" and contributed to his crushing defeat. It is a lovely irony that the Earned Income Credit was first enacted, below the radar screen of the national media, only three years later.

We have thus far explored two types of government intervention in the market economy. Prohibition of trading, we noted, is sometimes an expression of the absolute priority of one democratic value, such as equality in the case of voting rights, or public health in the case of cigarette sales to minors. In these cases, we deliberately subordinate both economic efficiency and conflicting democratic values, such as personal liberty. Taxes and subsidies, by contrast, often embody what Arthur Okun called "uneasy compromises" between political objec-

26. James Tobin, "The Case for an Income Guarantee," *Public Interest*, no. 4 (Summer 1966): 31–41, and Milton Friedman, *Capitalism and Freedom*, pp. 190–195. The proposal was given serious consideration by the first Nixon administration. The difference between the earned income credit and the negative income tax is that the former provides a stronger incentive to work at the very lowest levels of income, while the latter gives a lump sum credit to all and imposes a flat tax on all earned income.

tives and economic efficiency.[27] In fact, the compromises are often multi-sided, reflecting more than one political objective. The U.S. tax code, for example, displays, on the one hand, a desire of Congress to reduce inequality through the progressive income tax, which is compromised, on the other hand, by a desire to ensure "fairness" in sharing the burden of payroll taxes. In the context of welfare reform we have also seen that, without compromising the primary political objective of reducing poverty, it is possible in principle (though only imperfectly in practice) to improve economic efficiency and even achieve a secondary political objective—greater self-reliance.

A third type of government intervention holds great promise for correcting, at minimal cost, one of the major deficiencies of the market economy—its inability to economize on resources that are owned in common, such as the earth's atmosphere, oceans, and inland waters. I refer to the possibility of using the properties of markets to reduce pollution as efficiently as possible.

Most pollution control policies implemented since the enactment of the Clean Air Act in 1970 take one of two approaches. The first is to require the use of specific pollution control equipment, such as catalytic converters in automobiles in the early 1970s. The second is to set specific limits on the rate of emissions from a particular source, such as pollution per unit of fuel burned by an electric utility plant or an automobile. Both approaches have serious disadvantages. Requiring specific equipment can be a needlessly expensive way to achieve a desired result. For example, catalytic converters proved to be more expensive and less technically effective than making cars out of lighter materials and improving the efficiency of the combustion process itself. Setting limits on the rate of emissions from a particular source fails to take account of the wide disparities in the cost of reducing emissions from source to source. This is especially problematic for electric power plants, where pollution can be reduced by several means,

27. Arthur M. Okun, *Equality and Efficiency: The Big Tradeoff* (Washington, D.C.: Brookings Institution, 1975), p. 1.

including switching to cleaner fuels and adding filtering equipment (called scrubbers) to the smokestack. For plants close to the source of low-sulfur coal, for example, the cost of meeting emissions standards can be much lower than for others who must add a scrubber. In consequence, it has long been believed that the cost of complying with source-specific emissions limits is much higher than would be necessary to achieve any given regional or national target for aggregate reductions in emissions.

Economists solved these problems, conceptually, decades ago. By specifying a national limit on total annual emissions of a particular substance, let's say sulfur dioxide, and issuing tradable permits, a market will emerge that sets a price on the right to emit one ton of sulfur dioxide. Let's assume that the total amount of rights issued is less than the total amount of pollution that would be emitted without some remedial action. Every public utility can then ask itself the question: am I better off using the rights I am issued or selling them at the market price?

The answer is: I will sell my right to emit one ton of SO_2 if its market price exceeds what I can earn by producing as much electricity as I can generate while emitting one more ton of SO_2. But notice this: the calculation changes if I can produce more electricity for every ton of SO_2 emitted. So I have an incentive to look for the lowest-cost means of reducing my pollution per unit output. With tradable rights, the nation's utilities will minimize the total expenditure on reducing emissions to whatever level is established as the national target.

This is no mere theory: in 1990 Congress amended the Clean Air Act to establish just such a scheme for trading the rights to emit sulfur dioxide. The market for rights was established in 1993, and limits on aggregate emissions were established for every year beginning in 1995. The rights to pollute, called allowances, are dated by year. Unused rights can be banked for future use, but no borrowing from future allocations is permitted.

The operation and effects of this market have been thoroughly analyzed and documented in a study by Paul Joskow and other economists at MIT.[28] Suffice it to say that the market has worked smoothly. The annual emissions targets, which called for a one-third reduction from 1990 levels by 1997, were met in the aggregate, and every participating utility was in compliance. Nearly two-thirds of the reductions were achieved by switching fuels and just over one-third by installing control equipment. The MIT study estimates that, based on the evidence to date, the total cost of achieving the targeted reductions by the year 2007 will be approximately $16 billion. This is $20 billion less than it would have cost to achieve the same aggregate target by simply imposing quotas on each individual plant and not permitting the trading of rights.

One puzzle remains. How did such a rational and efficient means of achieving a political objective emerge from the legislative process? The MIT study suggests a serendipitous convergence of interests in 1989–90. The particular problem created by sulfur dioxide emissions was acid rain, which threatened destruction of lakes, forests, and associated species in the northeastern United States. Several attempts to impose stringent conventional regulations on SO_2 emissions had failed in Congress during the 1980s. But President Bush had campaigned on a platform of "looking to the market" for environmental solutions. He also had a summer residence in Maine, and his chief of staff, John Sununu, had been governor of New Hampshire. In the Senate, the majority leadership passed from Robert Byrd, from the coal-producing state of West Virginia, to George Mitchell of Maine. Presumably the coalition of liberal Democrats with a regional interest in eliminating acid rain and Republicans predisposed to a market-oriented approach was sufficient to defeat legislators representing coal-producing regions and Midwestern states with coal-burning power plants.

28. A. Denny Ellerman, Paul L. Joskow, Richard Schmalensee, Juan-Pablo Montero, and Elizabeth M. Bailey, *Markets for Clean Air: The U.S. Acid Rain Program* (New York: Cambridge University Press, 2000).

Perhaps I am guilty of excessive enthusiasm for rationalizing public policy. A partial welfare reform and one successful pollution-trading scheme do not necessarily foreshadow a revolution. Everyone knows, so the familiar argument goes, that public policy is not the product of rational design but the outcome of struggle between powerful interest groups. Those with interests to protect and money to spend will manage to subvert attempts at reform, and use them to reinforce and strengthen their power.

I can only respond that skepticism about the efficacy of democratic governance has long had a place in American life. But so, too, has optimism about the power of ideas to improve human welfare. I refer not only to the optimism of the founders. I refer also to the optimism of the freedom riders—black and white—who rode buses and led marches to integrate the South forty years ago. I refer to the optimism of the small and dedicated band of writers, naturalists, and lawyers who put environmental quality on the national agenda thirty years ago. On a smaller and more local scale, I refer to the optimism that has impelled many of the nation's urban universities to reorient and reorganize themselves to contribute substantially to the betterment of the communities that surround them.

The market is the most powerful instrument for improving material well-being yet devised by humanity. But it is an imperfect instrument that rewards individuals unequally and fails to economize on unpriced goods, such as clean air and water and the health of future generations. There is a role for democratic government to remedy the deficiencies of market outcomes, and there is also good reason to design remedies that achieve their objectives without compromising the incentives for socially productive activity that the market provides. That we have not done such a great job of this in the past should not deter us. There will be abundant opportunities for creative policy design as America confronts the challenges of the new century.

To reinforce this last point, I close with the words of Walt Whitman. I quote from the essay that we commemorate in the title of this lecture series—"Democratic Vistas": "America, filling the present with greatest deeds and problems, cheerfully accepting the past, . . . counts . . . for her justification and success . . . almost entirely on the future. Nor is that hope unwarranted. . . . For our New World I consider far less important for what it has done, or what it is, than for results to come."[29]

29. Walt Whitman, "Democratic Vistas," in *The Portable Walt Whitman*, edited by Mark Van Doren (New York: Viking Penguin, 1974), p. 317.